Collectible Fishing Reels

Carl Caiati

Schiffer Publishing Ltd

4880 Lower Valley Road, Atglen, PA 19310 USA

Dedication

This book is dedicated to the poor, lost souls of the Bi-polar Region. May they somehow extract some peace from their turbulent lives.

Published by Schiffer Publishing Ltd.
4880 Lower Valley Road
Atglen, PA 19310
Phone: (610) 593-1777; Fax: (610) 593-2002
E-mail: Info@schifferbooks.com
Please visit our web site catalog at www.schifferbooks.com
We are always looking for people to write books on new and related subjects. If you have an idea for a book please contact us at the above address.

This book may be purchased from the publisher.
Include $3.95 for shipping.
Please try your bookstore first.
You may write for a free catalog.

In Europe, Schiffer books are distributed by
Bushwood Books
6 Marksbury Ave.
Kew Gardens
Surrey TW9 4JF England
Phone: 44 (0)20-8392-8585
Fax: 44 (0)20-8392-9876
E-mail: Bushwd@aol.com
Free postage in the UK. Europe: air mail at cost

Copyright © 2003 by Carl Caiati
Library of Congress Control Number: 2002116447

Designed by Joseph M. Riggio Jr.
Type set in Bernhard Modern BT/Lydian BT

ISBN: 0-7643-1767-9
Printed in China
1 2 3 4

Contents

Acknowledgments

First things first; I must honor my debt of gratitude to the people who were most instrumental in assisting me in making the book possible.

Foremost, I want to thank Tom Greene of Custom Rod and Reel, Lighthouse Point, Florida. Tom owns one of the finest and best-known tackle shops in the southern United States, where he builds the finest custom deep-sea fishing rods in the world. A good friend and forthright gentleman, Tom is also an avid collector and boasts one of the finest collections of collectible reels. I can attest to that! Because of Tom, I was able to accrue an infinite number of photos pertaining to reels. His infallible expertise was of great value.

Of course, bundles of kudos to all the great writers of collectible material before me. They facilitated my research, as well as making the history of the reel enlightening.

The crew at Lesters Diner, Margate, Florida; writers have been known to write in their studios, bedrooms, in motels by the sea or at lakeside idyllic locations. This book was written daily in a diner, usually between the hours of nine and midnight. I was allowed a secluded, well lit table in the back with the waitresses plying me regularly with coffee or iced tea, as well as some great food. My particular thanks to my cherished manager, Suzi Spiro, and Robin.

Last, but far from the least, my dear friend, Ruth Levy, who put in hours of typing my material with true computer competence.

I have a penchant for surrounding myself with the best!

Foreword

Carl Caiati did his homework, but that comes as no surprise. If you know Carl, you can't help but marvel at his attention to the most minute detail in everything he does. Give him a project and he becomes totally absorbed in it. Let me give you an example. For relaxation, Carl builds four to six foot scale model ships. There are no kits and no plans. Instead, he researches the ship thoroughly before beginning the project. Then, he starts with the hull and creates each piece separately by hand until an entire ship model has been built.

As a long time professional writer who prides himself on copious research, Carl Caiati ranks as the perfect person to gather the most meaningful information ever assembled on antique fishing reels. Carl's goal was to go well beyond the handful of books on the subject. If you do nothing more than read his chapter on an overview of fishing reels, you quickly understand the history of fishing reels. Once one understands the development of reels and the timetable, the progression of fish catches and techniques make much more sense.

Tom Greene of Lighthouse Point, Florida, one of America's major antique reel collectors and an authority on them, had this to say. "The book is all-encompassing and the most thorough work ever done on the subject. It includes the history, date, manufacture, current value, and price ranges of sales. Primary coverage spans the nineteenth and twentieth centuries all the way to the present."

Color and black and white photos of many of the most important reels grace the pages of this book, aiding the identification and historical reference. Among them are Meeks, Milam, Vom Hofe, Meisselbach, Pflueger, and others. Simply looking at pictures of those reels gives one newfound appreciation for the skills and determination of anglers of those eras and the catches they made on that tackle.

This long awaited and much needed addition to angling literature comes at the perfect moment. In recent seasons, the number of antique reel collectors has mushroomed, with more joining the ranks every day. Consider, too, that people across the land are now focusing on old fishing tackle, and particularly reels, learning to their delight that these forgotten treasures have impressive values.

I personally applaud Carl for his unrelenting persistence in seeing this massive project through to its completion. This magnificent effort will stand the test of time as the primary reference book on the subject of antique reels. As you refer to it over and over again, I know you will join me in saying, "Thank you, Carl!"

Mark Sosin
Boca Raton, Florida

Chapter I
Fishing Reels – A Retrospective Overview

It can be an arduous if not fruitless task pinpointing the origin(s) of the earliest and more primitive fishing reels. At best, we can only estimate in backward glances, relying on historical footnotes to enlighten us as to the earliest inceptions of fishing reels.

As fly-fishing is keynoted as one of the earliest angling forms, it is innocuous to assume that the earliest reels were fly finishing reels. Onesimus Ustonson is credited with one of the initial designs when he fabricated his first specimen, a brass multiplier. The same concept was included in a kit of later manufacture, one of which was presented to King George IV around 1928 in London, England. The premier tackle maker of his day, he passed on his knowledge and business upon his demise in 1810 to his son Charles, who carried on until his own untimely death in 1816. The business then passed into the hands of Charles' wife, Maria, who carried on the tradition and manufacture of Ustonson reels throughout the mid-1800s. Though Ustonson utilized and made mention of the multiplying and reel stop mechanisms, he never took credit for their discovery. We can assume, however, that he was carrying on an age-old tradition, modifying and improving upon existing design theory of his day. In the last quarter of the eighteenth century, English offshoots of Ustonson's design came into general and widespread use amongst the swelling ranks of fly fishermen. These early reel designs and concepts made their way to the original American colonies and the Colonial period gave birth to a host of American fly fishermen as early as 1773, three years before the colonies claimed their independence from the mother country.

It has been accepted by historians that reels reached their first peak in popularity in the closing years of the eighteenth century. Prior, around the mid-eighteenth century, iron was predominantly used in reel structuring, in total reel fabrication or to reinforce the early wood reel renderings. The earliest reels sported one foot for rod mounting, but gave way to the double foot reel mounts as we know them today for more secure mounting. Very few early reel offerings are identifiable, as most were not signed and points of origin not designated

Though the early halcyon days of reel manufacturing hold a special interest for antique reel collectors, it is the nineteenth century that spawned a host of revolutionary collectibles that most intrigue reel collectors. The early 1800s gave birth to the first reel smiths, who fashioned their wares by hand, crafted from simpler metals available at the time that lent themselves to hand crafting and machining, utilizing simple machine tools that

prevailed in that era. Many early reel smiths fabricated their pieces by hand and utilized jewel movements as rotational pivot points. The pieces were also hand engraved and signed by individual craftsmen.

In the decade between 1800 and 1810, George Snyder designed and innovated the forerunner of the "Kentucky Reel," a bait-casting reel which was to revolutionize light tackle fishing. The same decade was the gestation period for many other Kentucky reel smiths of renown including Milam, the Meek Brothers, Sage, Noel Conroy, Hardman, and Clark and Shipley who fabricated their reels from brass and silver.

Bait casting reels were originally designed to cast minnows and similar live bait, hence the term "bait-casting reel." Contemporary bait-casting reels are primarily designed for delivering and working plugs on both fresh and saltwater, and are particularly effective when fishing for Bass, Pike, Tarpon, Permit, and similar fish frequenting lakes and saltwater flats. They are still often used in live bait delivery as well.

The nucleus of the bait-casting reel is its spool, which should be light in weight in order to rotate quickly and stop quickly to give the fisherman better line delivery and retrieval control. The spool must overcome inertia effectively while stopping quickly with minimum inertia, exemplifying the law of physics in which a body in motion tends to stay in motion, while a body at rest tends to stay at rest. A heavy spool would be more difficult to spin or stop. In order to minimize weight, the lightest compounds are utilized in spool construction. Spools of the nineteenth century fabricated from steel, German Silver, brass, and wood have given way to modern-day versions machined from such materials as aluminum, magnesium, and some of the tougher, more durable miracle plastics. Wood spool centers were used effectively in the nineteenth century, particularly in older tournament version reel models for their low weight value, which made them highly controllable.

Earlier vintage reels, particularly those of the early reel smiths, rotated on jeweled pivots or points. Though this method of spool axle retainment (the pivot point that holds the reel axle) and reel rotation has been replaced by modern ball bearing drive mechanisms, the old reels are classic pieces of jewel movement machining and operate as effectively as their modern counterparts.

Toward the latter part of the nineteenth century, "free-spooling" became a prominent feature of the bait-casting reels. In a free-spooling reel, the gearing and drive mechanism of the reel is disengaged from the spool, usually by depressing a lever or release prior to making the cast. This allows the reel to revolve easily and rapidly on its axis to deliver line at a more rapid and uninhibited rate. Most quality reels of today and yesterday incorporate free-spool mechanisms, whereas inexpensive bait-casting reels omit this necessary feature.

Toward the latter part of the nineteenth century and early twentieth century, sophisticated devices such as level winds and star drag mechanisms were incorporated into bait-casting reels, making them one of the most desirable reels with which to catch and manipulate fish.

As early as 1908, T. Williamson innovated a 9x multiplying reel which placed the handle in the center of the reel, confining it well inside the circumference of the reel, making the handle less vulnerable to damage. The Williamson design incorporated the first click mechanism even though Williamson did not utilize the click action in his own reels. The early multiplying reels (1905-1908) did exhibit some technical and operational shortcomings and toward the mid-1800s, single action reels took preference in a renewed shift back to single action reels. The early 1800s also gave rise to the Birmingham reel concept, considered the prototype of the fly reel as we know it today. One of the early Birmingham reels was produced by James Haywood in 1815. The Haywood reels were not true Birmingham reels, but actually old style large spooled multipliers and stop-locking single action types that the new style Birmingham reels were rendering obsolete.

New British Birmingham reels were manufactured cheaper and in great quantities due to updated manufacturing facilities made possible by the Industrial Revolution. The newer reels were constructed of brass, sans click mechanisms, decorative curved cranks with bone handles, and sported conventional reel-foot mounts. The reels also featured narrower spools that, though essential to both fly and bait-casting, gained wider acceptance in fly-fishing circles.

Toward the mid-1800s another refinement was instituted in the Birmingham reel–a raised check plate. The check plate was an internal disc housing on the back plate that also housed the click mechanism. The raised check plate allowed easy access to the fisherman for repairing, replacing, adjusting or oiling the working inside mechanisms of the reel without undergoing total disassembly of the reel. The elevated check plate proved to be a weighty additive, became unpopular around the 1870s, but was improved upon and modified and favorably reintroduced into the U.S. by lawyer-historian-fisherman Henry P. Wells. The new Wells design intrigued reel maker Julius Vom Hofe, who produced a similar version from 1889 to 1911.

In 1867 yet a new design was incorporated into the Birmingham reel in response to complaints that the reel's handle tended to interfere with and foul up line. To alleviate this problem, the handle was attached directly to the side plate of the drum. The revolving plate was the next step forward in which the handle attached to the revolutionary plate, eliminating the miniature windless principal of retrieval.

Another reel type very popular during the mid-1800s and manufactured well into the 1900s in quantity was the Nottingham reel, named for its city of origin, Nottingham, England. Primarily a free-running, massive wood type reel with steel reinforcement and mechanisms, the Nottingham reels were designed for river fishing, but were soon drafted for fly-fishing. While these reels were produced up to 1940, they emanate an antique quality that makes them favored collector items–not too expensive, as they are common and easy to find.

Though the Meek brothers were primarily interested in producing "Kentucky Reels," they were also instrumental in producing a number of the finest fly reels of the mid-1800s era.

On May 22, 1883, innovations were introduced to the Nottingham reel by David Slater; the new reel design became known as Slater's Combination Reel. The new design incorporated the metal pillars of a conventional reel with the exposed front rim styling of the Nottingham design.

Another popular reel design, the aerial reel conceived by Henry Coxon, also of the town of Nottingham, England, was subsequently sold to Samuel Allcock, who patented the design under his name in 1896. This design concept is historically attributed to Allcock, though other reel makers of his period copied and elaborated on his original idea.

The aerial reel was light in weight, about 3-1/2" wide, with a distinctive spoked drum; a bit fragile, but well suited for fly-fishing. The aerials were constructed of combined materials and were produced for a span exceeding fifty years.

The Sun and Planet reel was perfected by its inventor, Peter Malloch, and introduced in the mid-1850s. Malloch's innovative design feature prevented the plate or arm from revolving on the axis of the reel at the time the line was run out. The handle also served to retard line run-out as required. Many considered Malloch's creation a fly reel. It was most versatile and, however used, it was excellently crafted and a formidable piece produced from German silver and bronze, with a hard rubber back plate. The Sun and Planet reel was widely marketed (as a fly reel) by Abercrombie and Fitch.

Fly reels by Hardy are touted as some of the finest, and the company is world renowned for fly reel excellence. The Hardy Perfect is most likely the first model fly reel to incorporate ball bearings and an agate line guide. Today they rate as the most expensive fly reels, and some early vintage Hardy Perfects will fetch as high as $5,000 on the collectible market. Since their beginning in the 1880s, Hardy has pioneered at least twenty-five distinctive designs, though their most formidable offering is the "Perfect" model.

In 1886, August F. Meisselbach was granted a patent for a unique new reel, later to be known universally as the "Amateur" reel. The reel featured special petal shaped cutouts which assisted in drying out wet contained line, a thumb brake, and a click mechanism. Patent #336,657, which also featured a spool mounted crank knob and counterbalance, impressed A.G. Spalding and Brothers, and they became agents for the new Trout and Bass reels called the "New Gobebic Reels." August, known as "Gus," and his brother, William, produced these reels in quantity in Newark, New Jersey. Moving to larger quarters in the same city in 1888, they formed A. F. Meisselbach and Brothers in the Halsey Street area of Newark, already known as a mecca for fishing tackle manufacturers.

By the 1890s the company was sharing notoriety in reel manufacturing with their famous contemporaries, William Mills, Wilkinson, Conroy, Billinghurst, Orvis, Vom Hofe, Malleson, Chubb, and John Knopf.

In 1895 the Meisselbach "Albright" was introduced–a raised pillar type reel with a brass back plate mode available in three common sizes. A ventilated, improved version was also introduced in 1895, called the "Featherlight," and the design was adopted by Shakespeare, Pflueger, and South Bend, but the copies did not have the workmanship of the original Meisselbach manufacture. All the earlier versions of the original Meisselbach reel designs are considered fly, bass casting or trolling reels.

In 1902, Meisselbach introduced the first take-apart reel; innovative, beautiful, but not practical due to its rubber end plates which were prone to damage with repeated disassembly. The rubber end plate problem was rectified and the newer take-aparts, essentially the same in design but with a brass end plate, became an industry high point in reel design.

In the early 1900s, Pliny Catucci, an engineering genius credited with eighty-three lifetime patents, was employed by A.F. Meisselbach and Brothers, creating an amalgamation of talents that created some of the finest fishing reels in history. Their lower prices, coupled with their high quality, made them one of the leaders in fine tackle production and one of the major American manufacturers of bait-casting reels. During its production span of thirty-one years, the company inaugurated by "Gus" Meisselbach, became one of the productive giants of the angling and tackle industry.

In 1874, Charles F. Orvis patented his model 1874 trout reel with a narrow spool and perforated side plates to aid in fly-line drying. The 1874 is considered an American standard in fly reel design and it enjoyed sales for four decades after its inception. With the Billinghurst as the grandfather of American reels, the Orvis 1874 takes its place as the father.

The Billinghurst reel takes us a little further back in time than the Orvis. It was invented by William Billinghurst, a foremost gunsmith of his day. In collectible circles, the Billinghurst reel is known as the "Birdcage Reel," and was the fourth fly-fishing reel to receive a patent grant. Its forte was the ability to recover line as much as a multiplying reel and much quicker than standard single-action fly reels of the period.

The raised pillar design was yet another fly reel innovation credited by most historians to Hiram Leonard, while in actuality James Ross was responsible for the earliest version of a raised pillar reel. The first raised pillar reel to achieve success and nationwide popularity was produced as the Hiram Leonard version originally patented by Francis J. Philbook but with manufacturing rights assigned to Leonard as soon as the patent was issued. By 1900, Leonard design reels were turned out in quantity in the New York City shop of Julius Vom Hofe, who continued to produce Leonard-style reels up to the Second World War.

Mass production and the specialization of labor heralded by the Industrial Revolution allowed early mass producers of reels such as Hendryx, Vom Hofe, Chubb, Shakespear, Pfleuger, Heddon, and Meisselbach to flourish, offering unlimited quantities of inexpensive to medium priced reels for the mass tackle market.

The Golden Age of reel making seems to be the period between 1880 and 1900. In this decade, reels achieved the highest level of excellence and impeccable quality with materials and fittings turned on refined lathes. Reels were fine-fitted and assembled by hand. Earlier exponents of fine reels like Meek, Milam, and Conroy were also able to extend their reel crafting into this revolutionary era.

Some of the finest and most highly collectible reels turned out during the Industrial Revolution were by the Vom Hofe family. The patriarch of the Vom Hofe family was Frederick Vom Hofe, who sired five children, two (Julius and Edward) of which became mainstays in the family tackle business The family business was inaugurated in 1857 by Frederick, who was joined in 1860 by his first son, Edward, his second son Julius, and third offspring, William. Early Vom Hofe reels bear the stamp "F. Vom Hofe and Sons, Maker". Frederick retired in 1882, leaving Julius, who had built his father's reel making shop into a profitable business, in charge. Soon after, Edward established his own tackle shop featuring his own saltwater reels as well as some of his brother Julius' stock. The Vom Hofe reels were primarily of Nickel Silver and Ebonite, a hard rubber compound favored by the Vom Hofes. Edward soon expanded into the production of fly reels, creating seven basic models that became popular with fly fishermen and are much sought after by collectors of today.

The Vom Hofe reels are considered items of unsurpassed elegance and construction. They are the classics of their age and it is a consensus of opinion that Vom Hofe reels are to American angling, what Hardy reels are to British angling.

A wide spread surge in American tackle growth and sales took place in the period between 1900 and 1930. More select items, especially reels, were offered by such companies as Shakespeare, Pfleuger, South Bend, Horrocks-Ibbotson, Heddon, and numerous others. In this period, classified as the "Expansion Age," anti-backlash devices came into being, as well as level wind mechanisms and a very essential feature—free-spooling.

Just prior to the 1900s, the spinning reel was invented, utilizing a revolutionary new concept of line casting and retrieval following the guidelines of its creator, Peter Malloch. This totally new design concept was quickly accepted, and by the late 1920s the spinning reel was gaining worldwide popularity, which promoted worldwide sales. It was soon to become the ideal form of fishing, since the ease of operation, positive lure delivery and pickup made a fisherman out of the neophyte, who found it difficult to adapt to the more sophisticated manipulations and rigors of fly and bait casting equipment. With the advent of the spinning reel, the duffer could successfully fish, starting from "ground zero" with minimal experience. The structural and mechanical advantages of the spinning reel allowed simple mastery of all angling techniques, fresh and saltwater.

Due to the fact that there is no inertia to override at the beginning of a cast (as with conventional bait casting reels), spinning tackle allows the implementation of extremely light plugs and spinners to deliver the bait or plug in a more effective manner. Spinning reels are less prone to fouling than more conventional reels. Most spinning reels contain a skirted spool that covers the rotational housing, eliminating line snag that can be caused by line infiltrating behind the lip of the spool, hence tangling on the reel spindle.

The period from 1930 to 1950 spurred great technological developments in many forms of reels. Faster winding gear ratios were adopted; modern alloys and plastic working components were instituted, and all integrating parts were machined or cast on modern mechanized assembly lines. The spin casting reel, a design extension of the spinning reel and a new functional concept that overrode the casting reel in freshwater fishing, gained prominence in the fifties. The spin casting reel, unlike the typical "open faced" spinning type, features a reel enclosed in a cone-shaped or tapering cylinder. The casting action or line feed is controlled by a button that releases line tension while casting. The spin casting reel is most effective in tight or small area fishing situations and is very popular with bass and freshwater fishermen.

Today, there are no major breakthroughs in reel design, all contemporary offerings and offshoots of the basic fly, casting, bait casting, spinning, and spin casting counterparts that fishermen have been utilizing for decades.

Chapter II
In the Beginning

In the very early days of sport fishing, probably around the middle years of the eighteenth century, reels were simple and primitive. Their basic purpose was to crank line out and back to the enclosed spool when mounted to rods, preferably with a fish at the hooked end of the line. The weight of the baited hook pulled out the line. Popularized by the British in the eighteenth century, the first operational reels can be traced to the Chinese as far back as the twelfth century, AD.

The English reels were referred to as "winches." They were secured to simple rods with cord, clamps or screws. A retrieval handle or "crank" was integrated onto the spool, usually on the faceplate to facilitate hand rotation of the reel assembly. It was desired, as well as essential, that the reel should rotate as smoothly and freely as possible. Prior to fishing with the assistance of a reel, however crude, early anglers relied on a length of line tied to the end of a bamboo or flexible wood pole, a practice that still exists in backward countries and even by latter day country folk.

In 1682, Robert Nobbes describes in his chronicles a reel known as the "thumb" reel, an elementary spool rotated by the finger, awkward to say the least.

The first truly functional reel was advertised and marketed by Onesimus Ustonson way back in 1770. Ustonson continued to build reels well into the nineteenth century. Ustonson is also credited with innovating a geared reel, a bona fide three-to-one multiplier. Ustonson's basic design was improved and perfected by George Snyder of Kentucky in the early days of the Kentucky

reel smiths in the nineteenth century. Exceedingly few examples of reels attributed to Ustonon exist today and they are the rarest of all reel collectibles. Those surviving are true brass treble multipliers with the attractive engraved script: "Ustonson, maker to His Majesty Temple Bar, London". Many of his contemporary or later period reels are devoid of signature and identification marks.

References in history to the use of reels prevail through the late eighteenth century, so that it is innocuous to assume that after the inauguration of the working reel, it became the vogue to fish with a reel affixed to a rod. The fly reel is probably the most basic of reels and it is likely that early reels were fly casters, incorporating the basic simplicity that constitutes the fly reel of today.

When the British emigrated to the colonies, they still nurtured their own angling customs while importing reels manufactured in their mother country. The perusal of old history books in the embryo years of American angling attest to the fact that there were a host of colonial fly fishermen.

An advertisement in Dunlop's *Pennsylvania Packet* ascribes to a line of fishing rods and gear formulated and crafted by an Edward Pole of Philadelphia. This leads us to assume that Pole was also a probable early reel smith. Unfortunately, to date, no actual representative pieces of Pole's wares have surfaced. In fact, it is exceedingly difficult to ascertain what early unmarked reel samples are true eighteenth century reels since the majority of them are unsigned and unidentifiable.

Early unknown fly reels from an early Shapleigh catalogue.
Values: Inexpensive reels are worth about $25 each.

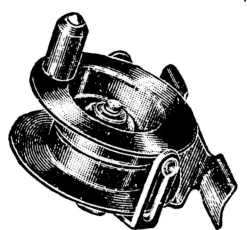
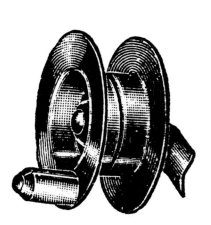

An old 3" direct drive fly reel of the late 1700s, early 1800s period. Origin and maker are unknown.
Value: $200-$400, depending on condition.

The hand crafting of reels was most likely exercised on a part time basis by clockmakers, silversmiths, and jewelers. Early reel renderings were home brewed by talented craftsmen who initially fashioned reels for themselves, friends or business associates. These "ghost reels" are highly coveted, though anonymous, by serious reel collectors regardless of their dubious origin or mystique.

Early example: Rear view of screw and pin method of securing side plates. Brass, origin unknown, early 1800s. This reel sports an extra long foot. Value: $400.

Mid-1800s brass single action, origin unknown.
Value: $300-$400, depending on condition.

Small early 1-3/4" brass reel with thumb drag. Unknown maker, date or origin. Value: $200.

Small, brass single action, mid-1800s, origin unknown. Value: $200.

Two more mid-1800s reels. Left: Peck & Snyder. Right: Hawks and Ogilvy. Value: left: $200; right: $400.

Extra small multiplier reel. German silver with extra long foot. Probably late 1800s. Value: $500.

Early brass multiplier, mid-1800s. Origin unknown. Value: $400.

T. H. Bate early multiplier. Custom handle, circa 1860. Value: $500.

The nineteenth century is considered the greatest era of tackle development, especially in the mid- to latter years. In the formative reel years of the nineteenth century, English anglers were prone to disapprove of the assumed superiority of multiplier reels and many anglers abandoned multipliers in favor of single action "Plain Pillar" reels. As the multiplying reel fell from grace in England, it was replaced with a new design concept: "The Birmingham Reel," so named for its birthplace, Birmingham, England. The Birmingham reel is considered the true ancestor and prototype of the fly reel. These reels were produced en masse in the early part of the nineteenth century around 1830. The initial versions were fashioned from brass and featured curved cranks called "sweep handles." Knobs were either of wood, horn or ivory. The foot was similar to the standard fly reel foot of today. Again, like the contemporary fly reel, the spool was narrow. These reels were adaptable to fly or bait casting but were primarily adopted by fly fishermen. Unfortunately, these early fly reel creations were virtually all unmarked, giving no knowledge of date or maker.

An early brass mini-casting reel. Unknown origin, mid- to late 1800s. Value: $500.

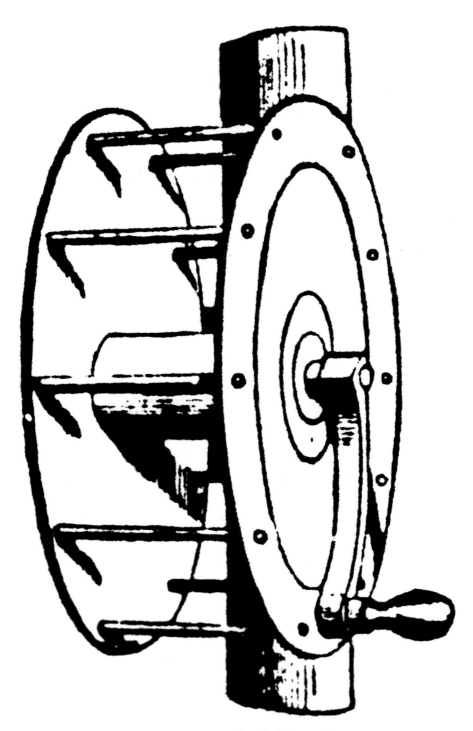

The Birmingham reel.

In the 1840s the Birmingham reels underwent a new transition. They now featured a raised check plate, a protruding round housing on the rear plate to contain a click mechanism. This facilitated lubrication without reel disassembly. By 1860, handle and knob were mounted directly to the spool side plate. It was further improved, utilizing a revolving plate fashioned from hard rubber and brass.

The Nottingham reels surfaced between the 1850s and 1860s, named for their city of origin, Nottingham, England. They were simple, free spooling wooden reels reinforced with metal braces. The woods used in their construction were mainly walnut and mahogany, outstanding in their durability. The free-running characteristics of the Nottingham reel made it essential to improved casting, allowing tackle weight to pull line from the spool with less tension. Various sizes were optional and the later, wider diameter reels became ideally suited to ocean and deepwater fishing. The Nottingham reels exhibit a beautiful antique-like quality with their fine-grained woods and exotic brass fittings. Though early forerunners, these reels were produced and used well into the 1940s. A premier Nottingham model designed by David Slater, an active tackle manufacturer, was introduced in 1883 and is known as "Slater's Combination Reel."

An assortment of Nottingham reels.
Values: Nottingham reels, most common,
values range from $100-$200.

A Nottingham apart, showing the gearing mechanism.

The Billinghurst Birdcage. Value: $1,600.

A most unusual concept in reel design is attributed to William Billinghurst who, in the mid-1800s, was considered one of the prime gunsmiths of his day. His 1859 Billinghurst Birdcage patent is considered by many to be the first American design fly reel. This revolutionary reel recovered line as fast as the then conventional multiplier and much faster than the single action reel of the period. Its open, skeletal construction allowed optimum ventilation for line drying. These reels are exceedingly rare and high in collectible value.

Peter Malloch was born in Perth, Scotland, in 1853. He is listed as early as 1878 as a fishing tackle manufacturer. He is known for his famous patent of March 25, 1880, the "Sun and Planet" reel, which is considered the forerunner or origin of the spinning reel. Excellent for bait casting, its advantage lay in the fact that when line was run out by a fish, the side plate remained stationary, with the handle providing braking action for runaway fish. His reels sold up to his death, after which his family took over producing reels up to the Second World War.

From the mid- to the late 1880s, there was a proliferation of reel issue by makers well known as well as unknown. This period was the golden age of reel making. Dr. Alonzo Fowler, an Ithaca, New York, dentist, plied the molding technology of his trade, producing a hard-rubber reel, for which he received a patent in 1872. The reel was known as "Fowler's Gem," exhibiting the first utilization of a hard rubber substance known as Vulcanite. The Vulcanite was too fragile, hence the reel diminished in popularity.

In 1869, the raised pillar concept materialized, spawned by James Ross and popularized by Frances J. Philbrook of Bangor, Maine. William Mills and Hiram Leonard, together with Edward Payne, also helped pioneer this new concept. The Leonard and Mills reels were eventually also produced as early Vom Hofe offerings in the Vom Hofe factory in New York City.

Malloch's Sun & Planet reel, front view. Value: $270.

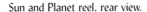

Sun and Planet reel, rear view.

Hiram Leonard raised pillar reel. Patented June 12, 1877. Value: $2,500-$4,500, depending on condition.

Three quarter view showing the raised pillar arrangement.

Early raised pillar German silver Vom Hofe type. No name or date. Value: $2,000.

Another anonymous raised pillar reel, early 1900s. Value: $400.

In 1864, the first U.S. patent was issued to Andrew Dougherty of New York for a braking mechanism to restrain a rotating spool from overruling line feed which tended to tangle lines. Dougherty's contrivance, controlled by a thumb lever, acted upon the revolving spool by means of a tensioning spring around a flange that decelerated the rotating spool. In 1885, in the United States, Winans and Whistler came out with a fixed spool reel providing resistance, which would eliminate backlash. Many years later, this unique concept, together with monofilament nylon, made the spinning reel a favorite amongst angling enthusiasts.

Charles F. Orvis of Manchester, Vermont, was another distinctive pioneer offering his renowned fly reel in 1874. It was of nickel-plated brass, very narrow and functional in design. It mounted on a fly rod vertically. It contained a click mechanism and two handle options were offered: a basic or counterbalanced S-shaped handle.

W.H. Talbot was another distinguished reel maker, though it is difficult to ascertain when he began producing reels. He was actively engaged in the watch and jewelry business (as were many of his reel making contemporaries) from 1887 until his demise, but devoted a full year to fabricating nothing but Talbot reels. He began his reel crafting in the early 1890s and in 1897 marketed his famed #3 casting reel out of Nevada, Missouri. He was one of the few reel smiths to use sterling silver in his reel construction, though his offerings were also optional in brass or German silver. The scientific aspect of reel construction was crucial to Talbot. His implementation of shouldered pillars allowed more rigidity and the adjoining screws fastening the side plates were less prone to loosening. His reels were exceedingly well crafted and accurate to tolerances of .0004 of an inch. An assortment of his fine reels were cataloged and marketed by Abercrombie and Fitch at the turn of the nineteenth century. It is speculated that his total output of reels exceeded 15,000, and his quality was equal to that of Meek and Vom Hofe. Unfortunately, the popularity of his products waned with the onset of mass produced reels, which dominated in the twentieth century.

Orvis Trout Reel. Value: $750.

The Tabot Niangua. Note the similarity to the Kentucky reels. Value: $605.

One of the earliest and most successful entrepreneurs of the reel making business was John Conroy. The House of Conroy has reserved a special niche in the annals of reel making. The establishment, located in New York, became one of the first reel making firms to mass-produce hand crafted reels. Conroy was one of the first singular mass producers of reels, with the company spanning nine decades. Most of the Conroy reels are iden- tifiable, stamped with maker name and origin. The firm was first established by patriarch John Conroy in 1830. Early reels marked John Conroy are rare and very valuable, fetching the highest collectible prices. The year 1840 marked the entry of his son into the business, when the firm was renamed the "J. & J.C. Conroy Co."

Early Conroy reels sported a curved enclosure on the left plate and a straight ball handle. With an eye towards quality, the Conroys were the leaders in the reel making business, utilizing at first brass in their makeup and then German silver.

In 1875, J. C. Conroy took on two partners and until 1881 the firm was known as Conroy, Bissett and Malleson. At this time the reels were stamped with the names of the three associates. In 1881 the firm was renamed again as "Conroy & Bisset" until Thomas J. Conroy took over the business. Today the products of the House of Conroy are much sought by collectors, and the older as well as the newer offerings fetch high prices from collectors.

Early Conroy with replacement ball handle, no name. Value: $1,000.

Early Conroy, 1830-1840. Value: $1,200.

Conroy Maker's stamped reel, 1850. Value: $1,200.

J. C. Conroy and Co.
stamped reel, 1860.
Value: $1,200.

Conroy early 1860,
German silver, single
action, showing the
raise click housing.
Value: $1,200.

Conroy single action type reel, circa 1860. Value: $1,200.

Conroy ball handle reel, 1860. Value: $1,000.

1860 Conroy stamped J. C. Conroy & Co. Value: $1,000.

S-handled, Conroy, Bisset & Malleson with restrainer pad, 1875. Value: $1,000.

Conroy, Bisset & Malleson, 1875. Value: $900.

The following images illustrate an array of reels designed
and marketed during the mid- to late 1800s period.

Reel produced circa 1885 under the auspices of Thomas J. Conroy. Value: $1,000.

Abbey & Imbrie after a patent of Vom Hofe dated Jan. 17, 1882. Value: $700.

Early fly reel circa mid-1800s. No established name or origin. Value: $500.

Unmarked German silver early multiplier, 1890
and up. Could be a Julius Vom Hofe. Value: $700.

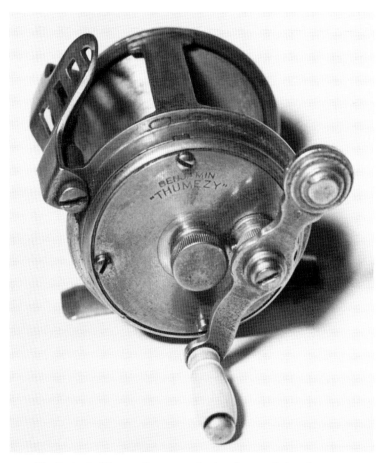

The Benjamin "Thumezy," very rare, few in existence, designed
in the late 1800s, marketed 1905-1915. Value: $1,200.

Small, two inch brass multiplier, mid- to late 1800s, origin unknown. Value: $600.

Small, brass, single action, circa 1880, origin and maker unknown. Value: $300.

Long foot early brass caster with drag tensioning, late 1800s, unknown. Value: $300.

Very early 1800s German silver, exposed click housing.
Unmarked but similar to Conroy. Value: $1,000.

The first automatic fly reel was invented by Francis A. Loomis and patented on December 7, 1880. He collaborated with James S. Plumb of Syracuse, New York, to form Loomis, Plumb and Co. to market the newly conceived reels in three sizes. In the mid-1880s the company was sold to Philip H. Yawman and Gustave Erbe, who re-designed and improved upon Loomis' earlier technology. The reel, constructed of lightweight aluminum, received a new gearing mechanism in 1888, making it more reliable in performance. The avant-garde key wound spring that was incorporated made the Yawman-Erbe fly reel popular and highly salable well into the first quarter of the twentieth century.

Julius Vom Hofe, New York, S-handle, German silver, late 1800s. Value: $500.

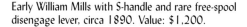

Early William Mills with S-handle and rare free-spool disengage lever, circa 1890. Value: $1,200.

Just at the close of the century, C. H. Wisner astounded the reel world with his handmade German silver free-spool bait casting reel. Very few of these 1899 patent reels exist and they are the rarest of reels. The reel features a free-spool release mechanism activated from the handle, the first of its kind. Also contained in the reel faceplate housing is a four-point rotary ratchet gear click switch. This is one of the most unusual and rare collectible reels.

Rod and reel combos prospered well into the 1940s but the origin dates back to 1864. On July 12th of that year, Thomas Cummings of New York was issued a patent for the first combination rod and reel. Two of the most renowned are the Streamliner and Hurd Supercaster. Manufacturers of these integrated units claimed that this configuration would eliminate back lashing but overruns would still occur. They had limited versatility, and interest for this type of angling device soon dwindled.

The highly innovative Yawman & Erbe automatic fly reel, the first of its kind patented on February 28, 1888. Value: $150.

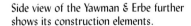

Side view of the Yawman & Erbe further shows its construction elements.

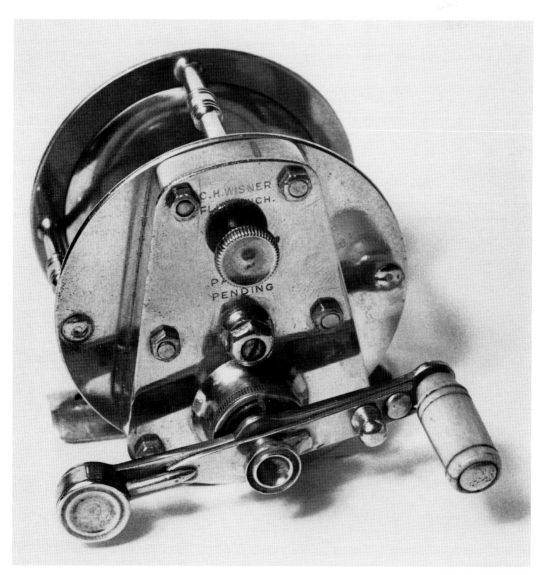

C.H. Wisner of Flint, Michigan, created and handmade a limited number of these classic reels. Value: $5,000.

The Hurd Supercaster, a novel combination of integrated rod and reel. Value: $200.

Very rare Holsman, produced 1890-1910. They can fetch up to $6,000.00 if found.

The Wolf reel, considered the first free-spooling reel, circa 1890. Value: $5,000.

Chapter III
The Kentucky Reel Smiths

In the annals of fishing reels, the formidable stand outs are the offerings of the Kentucky reel smiths. Amongst the famed reels are classic examples created by 1800s to 1900s notables such as B.F. Meek and Sons, B.C. Milam, G.W. Gayle, and G. Snyder. Their reels were considered the esoteric versions of their times, and today they are high in collectible appeal. The reels indigenous to the Kentucky locale were produced by craftsmen most adept at refined hand-crafting and early machining procedures. These individuals were, for the most part, locksmiths, silversmiths, watch and jewelry makers, with a few gunsmiths thrown in.

In the 1900s, reel making by hand and basic machining would give way to factory mass production as fishing as a leisure time pursuit grew in popularity.

The Bluegrass region of Kentucky spawned a proliferation of rivers, streams, brooks, and lakes with relatively few integrated large waterfalls, making the waterways ideal habitats for bass, which soon became chosen prey to the angling enthusiasts of the region. The major drawback in bass angling was the shortcomings of early rudimentary reels, which, in the early 1800s, did not deliver accurate or long-range casting. Enter the Kentucky artisans.

The Manufacturers

The Meek Reels

The Meeks are credited for establishing the Kentucky reel industry and considered the foremost proponents of ultimate quality reels. The principals of the Meek cycle of reels were Benjamin Franklin Meek and Johnathon Fleming Meek. In the 1830s, J. F. Meek established residence in Frankfort, Kentucky, where he thrived nurturing a successful jewelry business. In the same time period, the other Meek apprenticed to Thomas Robinson Ayres, a Danville silversmith, to study and learn the rudiments of jewelry and watch repair. In 1835 he relocated to Frankfort and aligned his services with brother Johnathon. A third party, Benjamin C. Milam, also an accomplished jeweler, came into the fold. One day, while the trio plied their trade, a customer came to the shop to have a crude reel repaired. Not satisfied with its design and function, the customer asked the partners to fashion a reel that improved on the crude and dysfunctional design of the customer's reel. The embryo reel smiths decided to give it a try, which necessi-

tated a sojourn to the town of Danville. This was the closest locale of a cutting machine capable of machining the wheels, which were an integral part of a casting reel. The first wheels were cut at the Danville facility with watch quality precision. The initial reels to emanate after the first try were so precise that word soon spread, plunging the Meeks into the fishing reel business. The Frankfort reels generated much acclaim and were soon coveted by serious anglers of the day.

Soon Benjamin devoted himself to the fabrication of reels, while his brother concentrated on watch making and repair. The earliest Meek model was fashioned after an earlier Snyder reel and was in production prior to Milam entering the scene. Milam joined the dynamic duo in 1849, and the company was re-registered as J.F. Meek and Co. As a partner in the firm, Milam concentrated solely on the production of reels until the company was dissolved and he continued on his own.

About seventy-five reels were produced by B.F. Meek before he extricated himself from the reel making partnership in 1853. The early reels bear a "Meek" stamp, while later renderings feature the stamp: " J.F. and B.F. Meek, Frankfort, Kentucky". The later stamp was still gracing the Meek reels in 1849.

In the fifteen year period in which they were produced, "J.F. and B.F. Meek" reels underwent periodic changes, constantly improving in quality and design. The initial reels were constructed of machined brass with minor or no enhancement except for custom or special orders of which there were few. Structurally, the head and tail plates were connected via five rods threaded on the ends and fitting into accommodating threaded holes on the opposite (tail) plate; basically a screw together type of assembly. Reels of the elementary period were cranked by S-shaped handles, the knobs of which were fashioned from ivory, buck or buffalo horn. A click mechanism was incorporated into the head cap in which a steel or quill spring, when activated engaged a pinion, putting the mechanism into a "click" mode. A vast improvement over the earlier and more primitive Snyder reels, the early Meeks also featured lapping gears machined from cast-brass stock.

A number of Meek brass and later generation German silver reels featured two-piece head caps in which a rim is attached to a disc. Most reels contained quadruple mechanisms. The No. 5 reel had a gear tooth ratio of forty-seven to twelve; most of the smaller reels favored quadruple multiplication ratios.

The Meeks created a superior product with their innovative designs, which were unique and superior in quality to any reels that were earlier conceived by other past reel makers. Their ingenious use of German silver pivot bearings and finely tuned interlocking brass and steel gearing helped inaugurate a machining revolution in reel making in the mid-1800s.

B.F. Meek & Sons – #3 Free Spool tournament model. Aluminum, circa 1900. Wooden spool. Value: $1,000.

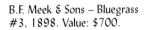

B.F. Meek & Sons – Bluegrass #3, 1898. Value: $700.

Three-quarters view of a three-handle tournament model showing the wooden spool, same as in the previous photo. 1882-1898. Value: $700.

Another #3 version with black knobs. Value: $700.

B. F. Meek & Sons Bluegrass #3 single knob, counterbalanced handle, 1898. Value: $700.

B.F. Meek & Sons #33 "Takapart" reel. End plates screwed off for maintenance. 1905. Value: $200.

The Milam Reels

With Jonathon reverting to the jewelry business as his main vocation, Benjamin F. Meek and Benjamin C. Milam formed a new company to produce reels under the auspices of Meek and Milam. Meek and Milam reels were in production in 1852. Until Milam's reels offered him sufficient income capability, it is innocuous to assume that the new partners continued watch making and repair, putting the newly established venture on a sound financial basis. In the period from 1853 to 1881, Milam was able to crank out about seven hundred reels, all of which bore the stamp: "Meek and Milam," Frankfort, Kentucky. After the partnership was dissolved in 1859, Milam continued in his clock and reel business while retaining rights to the Meek and Milam trademark. It was Milam's wise intent to capitalize on the widespread reputation garnished by the Meek and Milam reels, now exclusively machined from German silver (known today as nickel or nickel silver). Milam continued under the dual name until he discovered that his old partner, B.F. Meek, was moving to Louisville, Kentucky. To reestablish the Meek Co. at this point, the elder Meek took on his sons as partners.

In 1875, Milam's son, John, began apprenticeship under his father and the first reel constructed by John bears an 1880 date on the tail plate, but the elder Milam does not change the firm name to B.C. Milam & Son until 1890. The reels are not stamped B.C. Milam & Son until 1896. Up until 1896, the stamping remains "B.C. Milam, Frankfort, Ky." In 1896 Milam adds "The Frankfort Kentucky Reel" in an arch above "B.C. Milam & Son".

The 1850s and '60s give birth to some significant changes in Milam's reels. Introduced was a counterbalanced crank for better control. The size of the reels was somewhat reduced, probably due to metal shortages in the mid-1800s. This did not affect operational characteristics. A steel click spring for greater longevity became standard, replacing the older quill type. Optional brass or German silver construction was still offered, and a gold-plated finish became available in 1860.

One piece head caps were installed on the brass reels, then inaugurated on the German silver reels, consecutively incorporated into various other reel sizes. It is estimated that in the time frame between 1883 and 1928, 13,000 or more reels were produced by the Milams. By 1900, the son, John, was in full control, but Benjamin Milam passed away in 1904 and production declined, promulgated by the rise of competitive companies involved in the mass production of reels. The demise of John Milam in 1928 caused the firm to dissolve. The Milam reels forged a great namesake throughout their span of operation, which lasted about seven and a half decades.

Left: Early B.C. Milam reels were the same as late Meek and
Milam offerings. This is a #2. Value: $1,200.
Right: Another B.C. Milam reel trademarked with a Frankfort reel
arch. Also a #2 but with a differing crank.
Both circa 1800-1900. Value: $1,300.

B.C. Milam #3, 1896. Value: $1,200.

Two B.C. Milam reels #3. Note the different handles and no stamp on the S-handle model. Circa 1885. Value: $1,200.

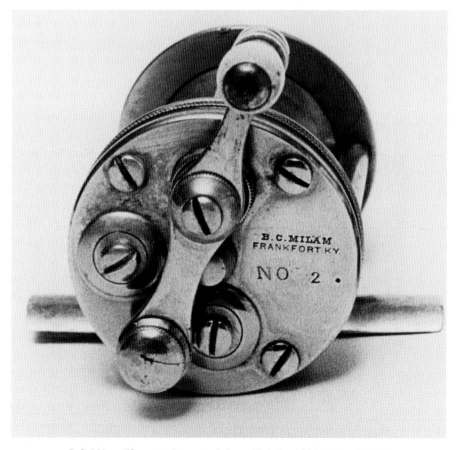

B.C. Milam #2 – straight counterbalanced handle, 1885. Value: $1,200.

Milam & Son screw-on counterbalance #2, 1898. Value: $1,200.

B.C. Milam #3 – note gracefully notched crank, 1900. Value: $1,100.

B.C. Milam & Son #6 Frankfort reel, with short crank, 1900-1910. Value: $5,000.

B.C. Milam #9 – a later casting reel with thumb tensioner, circa 1910. Value: $7,500.

The Return of B.F. Meek

Getting on in years, the patriarch, Meek, decided to embark on his new venture, the Blue Grass Reel Works in Louisville, Kentucky. Rejoining his sons after tiring of the watch business, B.F. Meek and Sons in 1904 markets a Blue Grass Reel which is marked "Blue Grass Reel made by B.F. Meek & Son, Louisville, Ky." Later the name is changed to "B.F. Meek & Sons, Louisville, Ky. – Blue Grass".

Spurred on by the acquisition of a Swiss spiral gear cutter, the elder Meek decides to implement helical gears into his future reels. Since no commercially made reels up to that time employed helical gearing, we can safely assume that B.F. Meek introduced the spiral gear concept to reel making. Earlier reels

utilized spur gears (teeth around the gear circumference) machined parallel to the axis of the gear blank. However, in the case of helical gears, with teeth spirally machined around the gear axis, there is increased tooth surface, larger spiral teeth are in more constant contact while meshing takes place. This type of gearing operates with increased smoothness while providing more wear resistance. These new reels were now turned out in quantity by Meek and his two sons, Pitman and Paul. A third brother, Sylvanus, joined the Meek reel making clan in 1884.

After the death of his sons, Paul and Pitman, Benjamin sold the company in 1898.

Yet another Bluegrass reel #3 by Meek with standard spool. Value: $800.

After the acquisition of B.F. Meek and Sons by J. H. Sutcliffe and Associates, two of its constituents, William Carter and James O'Connor, carried on the tradition of the firm, employing Sylvanus Meek and retaining the company name of "B.F. Meek & Sons, Inc."

The Blue Grass Reel works, backed by John Sutcliffe, started to mass produce the B.F. Meek & Sons reels, with William Carter creating inexpensive alternates to the Meek Kentucky Reels, which were also fitted with spiral gearing and German silver construction. Carter innovated the first mass produced Kentucky reel, the No. 33 "Blue Grass Simplex" which contained a tail plate that screwed on to a standard frame and was secured by pillars. This less expensive line featured a No. 33 and No. 25, both based on Carter designs but stamped "Blue Grass Reel made by B. F. Meek and Sons, Louisville, Ky."

In 1916, B.F. Meek & Sons was sold to the Horton Manufacturing Co. of Bristol, Connecticut. Most of the reels were labeled just "Meek", with the size of the reel also stamped. Above, in an arch, was written "The Horton Mfg. Co." and below "Bristol, Conn." Horton continued to mass-produce Meek reels up to 1936.

By 1916, B.F. Meek & Sons sold out to the Horton Mfg. Co., who added their name to the faceplate. Meek #2. Value: $700.

Meek #2 with wooden wide spool, 1916. Value: $700.

Meek-Horton #3 Bluegrass, 1916-1920. Value: $400.

Meek #3 double knobbed short crank version and altered design features, circa 1918. Value: $400.

Meek #4, long crank, late 1910. Value: $500.

Meek #5. The name "Meek" is deleted on the faceplate in favor of the Bluegrass stamp. Late 1910s. Value: $550.

Meek #7 Bluegrass, double handle. Note that now only three screws secure the end plates. Circa 1910-1920. Value: $600.

Bluegrass #10. Circa 1920-1925. Value: $400.

Meek-Horton Bluegrass Simplex, a budget
Kentucky reel, circa 1930. Value: $325.

Meek #30, extended click and drag
mechanism, 1920. Value: $300.

George Snyder

Though not a prominent Kentucky reel smith, George Snyder is credited with some early achievements in reel making, many of which were incorporated into the reels of his contemporaries. He was the first American reel smith to construct a multiplying reel. He was a silversmith and watchmaker by trade, and made his first reel around 1815 for his own sole use. Before his death in 1841 he manufactured a dozen or so reels. A number of Snyder-style reels were made by his sons, John and Charles. In comparison to issues of other Kentucky reel makers, the Snyder output is sparse. A typical early Snyder reel has the initials "G.S." on the bridge of the reel. The reel is assembled with three rivets mounting the reel foot to the bridge, and the bridge secured to the tail plate via a peened lug and then fastened to the head plate by two screws. Snyder employed a gracefully curved crank, and the gear train offered quadruple multiplying.

Snyder reels are amongst the rarest and most expensive finds. Later Snyder reels are stamped "J. & C. Snyder".

George Gayle

Gayle, a contemporary of B.F. Meek, was born in Frankfort, Kentucky, June 3, 1834. He served as an apprentice to the Meeks for a short time, after which he joined the jewelry-making firm of Worham P. Loomis, managing the business until Loomis' death in 1870. In 1882 he commenced reel making with his son Clarence. The earliest Gayle reel of which we are aware is a brass unit. The head plate is stamped "George W. Gayle & Son", but its fabrication is attributed to son Clarence. The Gayle reels marketed by the craftsmen are assumed to be the first to use rubber side plates, making the reels lighter and quite attractive. George Gayle passed away in 1896 and his son took over the manufacture of the Gayle-style Kentucky reels, introducing a new improved version in 1897. It was an all-metal reel much like the traditional Kentucky reel offerings, but with a raised gear box. In the 1880s, raised gear boxes started to become quite common. By 1899 Gayle was fabricating in German silver and in 1901 in aluminum as well. Though many early Gayle reels were produced, they are very hard to find. The company did produce reels well into the twentieth century and in the 1920s and '30s, many distinctive Gayle reels were produced with hard rubber (Bakelite) plates.

The aforementioned Kentucky reel smiths were the giants of their time. A number of lesser known reel smiths surfaced in the same era, such as: W.B. Conery, Thomas Dalton, James Deally, Frank Fullilove, Jacob Hardman, James Sage, Granville Medley, and William Van Antwerp. However, their output was meager and they are not acknowledged as great artisans or innovators.

The Talbot Meteor, first decade twentieth century; a common Talbot. It came
in grey finish, 2" diameter end plates, pyralin handle. Value: $300.

Talbot Niangua, knurled sides, #3 size, premiered in 1903. Value: $400.

Talbot Comet, released in 1910 in German silver, attractive knurling, straight counterbalanced handle. Value: $400.

Talbot Star, introduced in 1915, a budget Talbot without the options of higher priced Talbots. Value: $300.

Chapter IV
The Vom Hofe Family
of Fine Reels

Of all the refined reel makers, none have attained the excellence of aesthetic beauty like the Vom Hofe's. Sharing the same era as Thomas Conroy, the first prolific fabricator, they conceived reels that attested to their roles as foremost artisans. Conroy himself offered many of the Vom Hofe reels in his catalog through a major portion of the nineteenth century. The Vom Hofes also fashioned reels for other major tackle firms; their morphologic appearance typical of Vom Hofe styling, construction, and elegance. In many instances, the Vom Hofe trademark was not inscribed on the faceplates.

The Vom Hofe reels were to bait and surf casting what the Hardy reels were to fly casting, though Julius and Edward made many fly reel contributions to the anglers' market.

The earliest model Vom Hofe's were primarily of brass or German silver, but infinite notoriety was gained for the magnificent models embodying both hard rubber (then known as Vulcanite) and nickel silver. The family's legacy included classic reels: distinctly beautiful, highly functional, smoothly performing pieces.

Patriarch of the family, Frederick "Fritz" Vom Hofe, entered the U.S. as a German immigrant in 1847 settling in Brooklyn, New York, in a small ethnic area known as "Little Germany." The following year, Fritz Jr., Julius, and Edward ("Ludwig") followed suit and settled in the same locale, housed by father Frederick. Frederick's first reels were cruder than Conroy's, and for the most part unmarked. Early Fritz reels are identified by a bearing cup on the left side plate, more exaggerated than the cups on Conroy models. The circular side plates are also identifiable by a circular indentation around the circumference of the bearing cup. The unique feature of the bearing cup was that it could be easily removed to facilitate oiling. It is assumed that changes in the design between 1857 and 1867 included the introduction of the S-shaped handle, a distinct feature on many of the Vom Hofe family reels. A special main gear bridge included on the reels was patented by Julius on November 26, 1885. In the late 1880s the reels were also exhibiting the first practical use of hard rubber, a feature very quickly adopted by other reel smiths, including brother Edward.

Edward was the first of the family to leave the fold to strike out on his own with his own line of reels. Julius remained with his father, re-establishing the original firm as F. Vom Hofe & Son, supplying other tackle outfitters as well. Reels inscribe with the F. Vom Hofe & Son marquee ad is considered to be the rarest of the family's reel output. When Frederick retired in 1882, Julius continued the business but began using his own name. He mass-produced reels using the stamp: "Julius Vom Hofe-Maker".

Julius was an ingenious inventor and creator, holding many patents for revolutionary concepts. Julius made reels for Thomas Conroy, as well as for William Mills, Hiram Leonard, Abercrombie & Fitch, and Abbey & Imbrie. The reels farmed out from Julius carried his name and, on occasions, the name of the retailer.

Julius designed one more crucial series of reels before his death in 1907. As afterthoughts based on the New York design named the "Silverking" series, the faceplate contained a rim control lever to actuate a tensioning and click device originally patented by his brother, Edward, and a right-hand lever, also mounted on the faceplate, controlled a free-spooling mechanism. The latest Julius renderings were not only objects d'art, but perfection personified.

Early Julius Vom Hofe, extra long S-handle, German silver, circa 1857. Value: $1,500.

Early Julius Vom Hofe, S-handle and sliding oil cap, circa 1865. Value: $1,500.

Early Vom Hofe, no-name. Possibly Fritz Vom Hofe; early
spin off on Conroy style, circa 1857. Value: $500.

Early Vom Hofe with click-button and tensioner; German silver, 1900. Value: $750.

Early Edward Vom Hofe, 1865 to 1875. Value: $1,000.

No name, attributed to Julius, who produced a number of
raised pillar casting reels, 1888 patent. Value: $1,000.

Two smaller Julius Vom Hofe casting reels. Note the uncommon handle on the reel on the
right, differing from the traditional S-handle, circa 1900. Value: left: $125; right: $75.

Left: Early Julius Vom Hofe, no name. Right: similar bait caster by
Julius, dated November 17, 1883. Value: left: $300; right: $200.

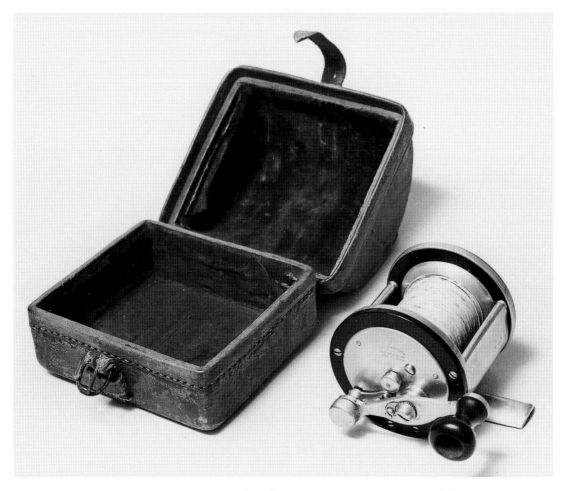

Rare early Julius with extra long foot. Original case adds to the value. Value: $700.

Julius, dated 1885. On the collectible market they are available in quantity. Many utilized brass as metal pieces. These can be purchased for $150.00 to $200.00 in mint condition. Value: $150.

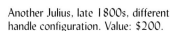

Another Julius, late 1800s, different handle configuration. Value: $200.

Edward plied his own business in earnest in 1867, utilizing his older brother Julius' patents on his reels. Some of Edward's earliest reels credit Julius' patent and incorporate Julius' swinging oil-port design, which then became part of the Edward Vom Hofe trademark. At their inception, Julius' patents and innovations were tantamount to making all other New York-style reels obsolete. By 1870, Edward's reels sported rim brake levers on the faceplates, whether of brass, hard rubber or German silver. They were state-of-the-art for the period and for decades to come.

From 1867 to 1901, Edward began developing high quality larger saltwater reels with highly advanced drag mechanisms, a significant advance for the manufacturer. One particular reel, the 621, fantastic for the control of fast fish (a 9/0 size red) was produced in the thousands. An output of specially designed trout and salmon fly reels was also created and successfully marketed.

We can only generalize as to whether the Vom Hofe's first initiated the star-drag mechanism. An early fitment of a Vom Hofe star reel can be found on the 521 size 9/0 model. Although the star-drag concept was claimed by Joseph A. Coxe, there are no early Coxe star-drag reels to substantiate the claim. Edward does lay claim to the invention of the free-spool mechanism, but history does not attribute this feature solely a Vom Hofe creation.

In the twenties and thirties peak production years, Edward turned out a plethora of reels of all types and sizes with short, thumbwheel levers protruding an eighth of an inch above the plate, indicative of reels made prior to 1916. If a Vom Hofe reel contains a handle-nut fitted with a ball-oiler (spring loaded) it was most likely manufactured after 1920.

In 1939, the Edward Vom Hofe Co. was sold to Ocean City of Philadelphia. Ocean City continued to produce Vom Hofe salmon reels until they ran out of parts acquired from the Vom Hofe acquisition. In 1940, the Vom Hofe line was dropped and Ocean City continued producing their own line of reels which could not compete with the Vom Hofe standard, either in appearance or quality.

Custom built Edward Vom Hofe. Rare
4/0 with double German silver side
bands on front plate. Value: $1,000.

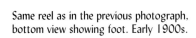

Same reel as in the previous photograph,
bottom view showing foot. Early 1900s.

Left: Edward Vom Hofe narrow spool 4/0. Right: 501
Edward 6/0, 1896. Value: left: $400; right: $750.

Edward, Model 570 Wahoo 1/0 narrow spool tak-a-part, 1916-1924. Value: $750.

Edward, Model 423 2/0, 1910-1920. Value: $1,200.

The Vom Hofe Family of Fine Reels

Edward "Restigouche" #423, a 4/0 salmon fly reel, circa 1910. Value: $1,200.

Another Edward 423 in size 3/0. Original leather case is shown. Value: $800; with case: $1,000.

Edward 621 tak-a-part, 9/0, 1902 patent. Value: $600.

Edward model 722 14/0. This reel is in mint condition, hence valued at $10,000.00. Very rare, 1910-1920.

Edward model 491, size 1/0, 1900. Value: $500.

Late 1800s Julius Vom Hofe, German silver, raised pillar salmon fly reel. Hard rubber faceplates. Value: $800.

Edward Vom Hofe model 423 with presentation case, 1900-1910. Value: $900.

Chapter V
The Twentieth Century

The twentieth century, spurred on by the industrial revolution and refined mass production techniques, gave anglers a proliferation of fine reels based on innovations of the earlier nineteenth century reel makers. Companies such as Pflueger, Shakespeare, Heddon, Meisselbach, and South Bend earnestly began to produce top quality reels in quantity. Level wind and improved drive mechanisms added to the charisma of the reel as the foremost and most significant entity of fishing.

For comparison, we can study the level wind on the 1915 Shakespeare (top) as opposed to the modern mechanism on a 1999 Garcia Ambassador™ reel.

Heddon 415 level wind designed by Jack Welch in 1915. Value: $3,000.

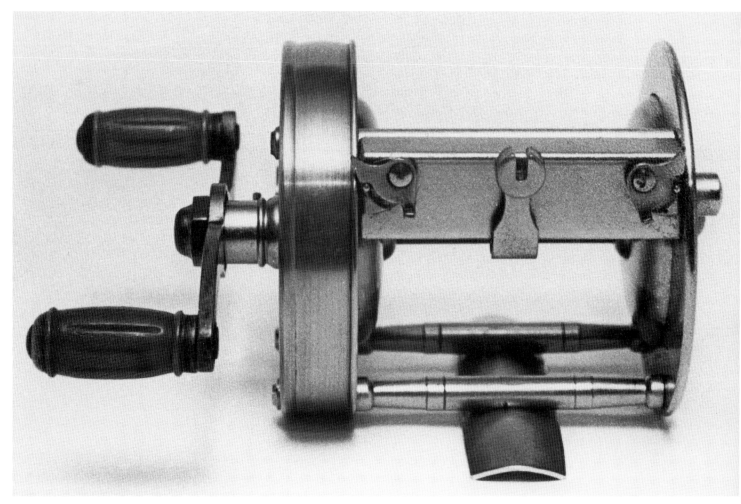

Early twentieth century (Supreme) tournament caster. First Pflueger level wind, designed by William Shakespeare. Value: $750.

Two reels designed by Welch; a left and right model, very, very rare (1918). Value: left: $1,200; right: $2,500.

Early drag retention concept: a leather thumb tension.

Drives and gearing were also improved upon to upgrade performance and all around dependability.

The refined inner gearing of a Vom Hofe "Wahoo," size 1/0.

Reel Manufacturers

The William Shakespeare Co.

As a formidable and still active tackle business, Shakespeare has been in existence for over a century; longer than any other reel manufacturer. William Shakespeare began his venture into tackle back in 1896 and is credited as the first reel entrepreneur to patent a level wind reel as far back as 1897. The reel, designated the "C" style, featured a dual worm-drive level wind, handmade with tolerances less than 1/1000 of an inch, which remained in production until 1902. His second reel was a quadruple non-level wind unit, which was inaugurated into his catalog in 1901. Shakespeare himself referred to the creation as the "rubber standard reel." It was, however, short-lived and after some major re-tooling in 1902, the original C-style reel was back on the bench, joined by three newer reel versions in three widths and nine sizes.

The three new reels, which added reel industry status to the company, were: the "Standard™", (*We use the ™ symbol for the products of any company that is still in business or now owns the products of another company. That helps keep you safe from any claims of copywrite infringement from the firm. If you see any other firms currently active in the book whose wares do not have the TM beside the name in its first appearance please mark them. Thanks.) differing its predecessor of 1901, the "Service™", a basic inexpensive reel, and the "Professional™", a German silver rendering of the "Standard". This roster of reels remained in the Shakespeare line till 1910, when they were replaced by the "Marhoff™" style winding mechanism utilizing a single worm-drive for line alignment.

In 1925, Shakespeare introduced the famed "Beetzel™" model after a patent assigned to the Redifor Rod and Reel Co. of Warren, Ohio, which was initially issued around 1908. It was considered, at the time, a perfect casting reel. Outwardly cloned, other Beetzel models were marketed by Redifor and Pflueger. It is readily assumed, however, that virtually all Beetzels were machined by the William Shakespeare Corporation.

Since its inception, Shakespeare (originating out of Kalamazoo, Michigan) has been most productive in spawning a myriad of fine quality reels, continuing to this day. The early reels up to the 1930s are considered prime collectibles; many types and models are readily available in the reel marketplace.

Early German silver casting reel with thumb control, possibly an early twentieth century William Shakespeare (unmarked). Value: $200.

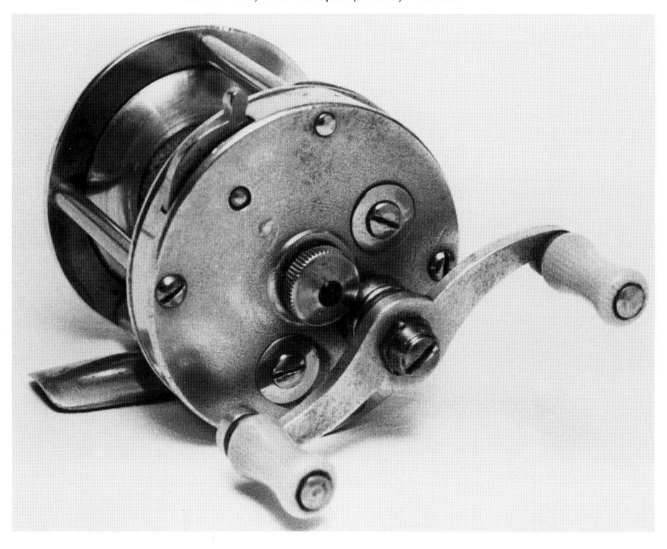

Early William Shakespeare turn of the twentieth century reel. Note knurled drag adjuster. Value: $250.

Shakespeare tournament #1740 free spool reel. Value: $110.

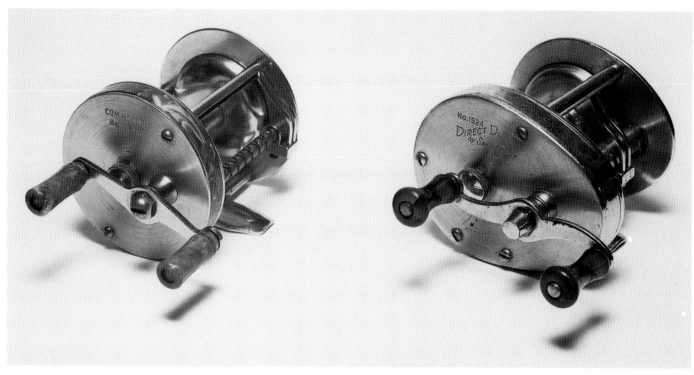

Left: Horrocks Ibbotson "Commodore" produced by William Shakespeare.
Right: Shakespeare Direct Drive #1924. (Circa 1920s.) Value: left: $150; right: $30.

Shakespeare #370 with star-drag mechanism. (1920s.) Value: $50.

Earnest F. Pflueger Co.
(Enterprise Mfg. Co.)

Considered the first of the mass production tackle companies, by 1900 Pflueger offered an ample one hundred and twenty-six-page catalog. At the turn of the century they began to seriously produce reels and, after 1930, concentrated on reel output.

On December 27, 1895, Earnest Pflueger created and patented the first hand reel. It resembled a line dryer, but, for all intent and purposes, served as a primitive but effective reel, a one-off special.

(No Model.)

E. F. PFLUEGER.
FISHING REEL.

No. 560,925.

Patented May 26, 1896.

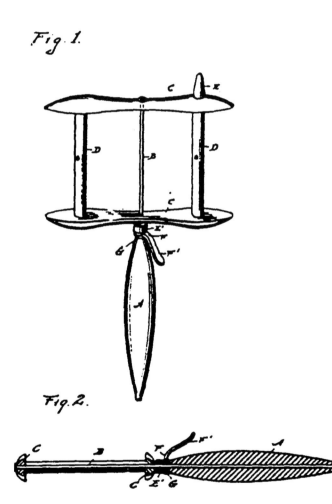

Fig. 1.

Fig. 2.

WITNESSES

INVENTOR

Pflueger's first patent for a hand-wind reel.

Pflueger, like his contemporary Shakespeare, was a staunch advocate of level wind features and incorporated them on his earliest reels. He also played around with drag mechanisms, which were for the most part primitive in the early 1900s. To regulate casting speed while minimizing thumb burn, early Pflueger reels mounted a leather thumb piece such as exhibited in the Pflueger 1885 Inter-Ocean reel. (See the photo of the early drag retention concept at the beginning of this chapter.)

In 1909, Pflueger dominated the reel market, offering over forty models of reels in all types and configurations, comprised of fresh and salt water casting reels, and even fly reels ranging from German silver and rubber versions, to machine punched simpler versions. In 1902, even a couple of Kentucky-style reels were produced: A first model "Akron™" and a machine polished version of the "Akron" named for the factory's home base in Ohio. By 1907, the Pflueger catalog boasted over fifty reel models.

Though the Pflueger factory turned out a plethora of reels between 1900 and 1915, the very early reels are not readily discernable as Pflueger issue, since the major output in the first decade were unmarked. There is also an aberration in model numbering, with some reels exhibiting exceptions to logical order. The cardinal rule was that the first to the three digits of a total reel number designated the specific design, while the last digit corresponded to the reels size. In the latter teen years of the early twentieth century, Pflueger formally assigned names to his reels to further aid "distinguish-ability." Minor changes were made to many reels periodically and many variations on reel types are to be found.

In all, the best quality was offered to all anglers. The Pflueger reel stock was mechanically sound, well plated, and unstinting in ornamentation. Later models, like the Pflueger "Rocket™" (#1355), implemented star-drag mechanisms, which soon became the accepted standard and are still used to this day by many manufacturers. In the 1960s era, Pflueger was sold to the William Shakespeare Corporation, its major competitor that also had its origin in the gay nineties.

The Pflueger "Worth." Value: $155.

Early Pflueger "Supreme," 1907 patent. Value: $750.

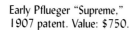

Pflueger "Redifor" featuring anti-backlash. Value: $130.

Pflueger "Capital" with early star-drag. Value: $75.

Pflueger model by Vom Hofe, 1900. Value: $150.

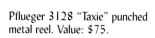

Pflueger 3128 "Taxie" punched metal reel. Value: $75.

Left: Pflueger conventional Supreme early version. Value: $750.
Right: Pflueger Oval Supreme. Value: $50.

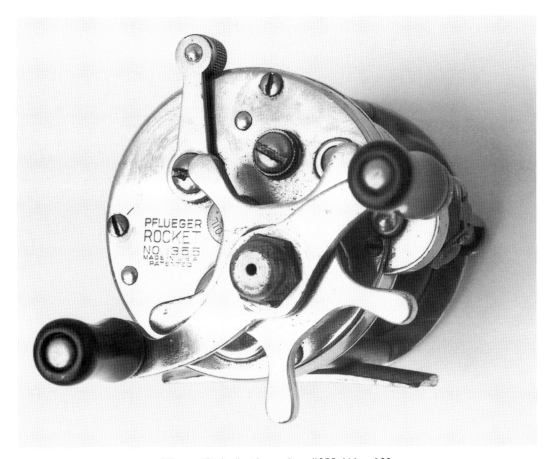

Pflueger "Rocket" with star-drag #355. Value: $60.

View of the Pflueger Supreme showing the Pflueger level-wind mechanism. Value: $50.

A.F. Meisselbach & Bros.

August F. Meisselbach was an avid and prolific angler. "Gus," as he was called, was born in July of 1865, but was preceded by his brother William who entered the world earlier in July of 1859. Together the duo created a facility that was destined to create some of the best mass-produced reels in the annals of reel history.

The Meisselbach brothers were offspring of German immigrants who settled in the town of Newark, New Jersey. Their father, Wilhelm, was an accomplished machinist, who readily taught his trade to the siblings. Their love of fishing gave the boys the impetus to put them on the road to reel history.

The brothers never aspired to compete with the ever-popular Kentucky reel smiths, but were dedicated to producing high quality pieces that the average working man could afford. In 1886, at the age of twenty, Gus obtained a patent for the famed "Gogobic" reel, so named by A.G. Spaulding, who first introduced the reel in their Chicago catalog. The introduction of Gus's new reel by Spaulding guaranteed the fledgling reel maker a thirty-year career as one of the most significant reel designers in the country.

With the inception of the "Allright" and "Featherlite" reels in 1896, the Meisselbach Co. moved to more expensive quarters on Newark's Prospect Street. Until the turn of the century, the Meisselbach boys had no interest relative to producing multiplying casting reels, but due to increasing demands, were forced to create one of their own. Soon they were manufacturing their infamous Tri-Part and Tak-A-Part reels, which easily became the most popular casting reels in the country.

The unique feature of the Tak-A-Part was that it could be disassembled quickly and easily by screwing off the endplates, eliminating the usual assembly screws that held virtually all casting reels together. Servicing, reel repair, and oiling now became a lessened task. No more lost screws and thread stripping.

On a 1900 fishing trip, the Meisselbachs met up with Pliny Catucci, an astute Italian immigrant born in Rome in 1869. Migrating to the United States, Catucci began his working career as a journeyman machinist. By the time he reached the age of forty, Catucci had established himself as an ingenious, practical, and innovative mechanical engineer. Gus and William quickly recognized Catucci's creativity and savvy and offered him a job, which he readily accepted. With Gus, William, and Pliny on the "A-Team" a free spool system was devised, which was applied to the Tak-A-Part reels that were produced for over twenty years. Other patents were consecutively issued to Pliny for automatic and salt-water reels, which he amicably assigned to Gus and William in return for stock options in the company.

In 1912, the trio formed the Meisselbach-Catucci Corporation. The origination did not however engage in reel production until the Meisselbach brothers retired. For all intents and purposes, the reels produced under the auspices of the Meisselbach-Catucci Corporation are specifically Catucci products. Some of the significant Meisselbach reels can be seen in the color section of this book.

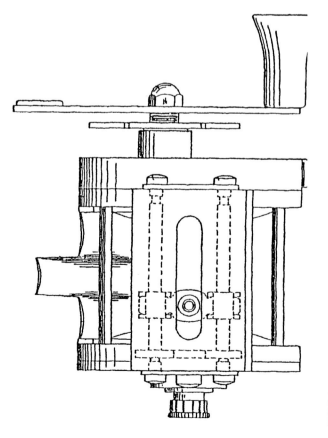 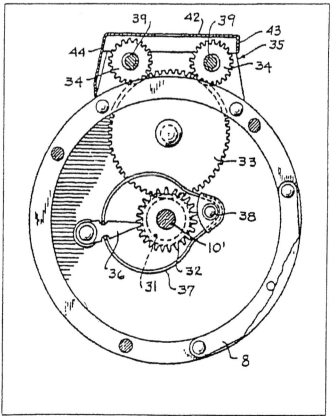

Pliny Catucci's last reel.

South Bend

A prime tackle manufacturer, South Bend began formulating casting reels in 1912. Their reels were known as "America's Blue Collar Reels"; the company offered quality at reasonable prices, providing the common man with a financially acceptable leisure-time pursuit.

South Bend's major claim to fame was their patented anti-backlash bail, which served as part of the firm's trademark. The first anti-backlash reel was introduced circa 1911. Advertised as model 1131, the number did not appear on either the face or back plate. The innovative reel contained only four moving parts: A wire bail frame, a drag lever with associated rubber-tipped brake pad, and a drag spring adjusted by a screw. This system was applicable to various reel models for over five decades. Threaded over the bail frame's main post and over the wire's leading edge, line tension reacted on the bail lifting it up, moving the brake pad away from the inner lip of the spool. The upward swing of the bail (about ninety percent) was controlled by a pin protruding a quarter of an inch from the spool side of the head ring. This basic but effective system allowed free-spooling for optimum casting. When bait hit the water, line tension slackened, bringing the brake pad into play, pressing on the inner lip of the spool. According to screw adjustment, brake contact with the spool slowed the motion of the spin. If a good-sized fish made a sudden all-out run, the reel would turn freely till the fish tired or stopped, activating the brake, thus circumventing backlash. The reel was constructed of German silver and the spool spun on solid Phosphor-Bronze bushings.

The first anti-backlash reel sold for a mere $7.50; up to the mid-thirties, South Bend reel prices never exceeded $10.00. In 1927, the company introduced the "Hummer" and after the war, the "Smoothcast" followed by the "Oreno-Matic". By the late thirties there were a proliferation of South Bend reel models. The 2500 ABL and the 1300 "Super" were claimed by anglers to be the finest reels ever released.

There are many variations of South Bend reels making the availability of types and models astounding. South Bend remained in business for over five decades.

Left: A Pflueger "Summit."
Right: A South Bend 350 anti-backlash.

Close-up of the South Bend 350. Note level-wind bail mechanism.

South Bend "Oreno" featuring star-drag and leather tensions. Value: $50.

James Heddon & Sons

Another giant in the reel and tackle industry was James Heddon of Dowagiac, Michigan. Heddon also gained notoriety for their fantastic lures, which dominated the artificial bait field, adding to the company's source of revenue for years to come.

Heddon began by plying the reel wares of other manufacturers such as: Meek, Meisselbach, and South Bend. In 1917, Heddon & Sons began producing reels on their own. This was made possible by the acquisition of two men who made reel history. The two constituents were James Carter from Meek and Jack Welch. Carter was an innovative reel craftsman, holding four patents for unique reel concepts while in the employ of the Meek family. Welch was an articulate designer who was to perfect many of the level wind characteristics applied to Heddon reels.

The first models offered by Heddon were the #30, #35, and the #40, quite similar to Horton, Meek, and Bluegrass reels. The major difference between the Heddon and Meek style reels was the number of pillars securing the frame. Carter decided that the four-pillar configuration (as opposed to Meek's five) was superior as one less pillar minimized the problem of removing backlash buildup from the spool. Carter instituted a double-knob crank, replacing the former counterbalanced handle.

Heddon sold Carter reel models up through the 1920s. The second decade of the twentieth century was a big turning point

for Heddon as Jack Welch was made superintendent of the Heddon factory. Welch was formerly employed by Carter at B.F. Meek and Sons, and for a short period by Talbot. One can easily discern the Talbot influence on subsequent Heddon reels produced under Welch's supervision.

Heddon marketed three new models in 1920 of Welch design: the 3-15, 3-24, and 3-30, all in a size 3. The 3-24 and 3-30 were carried in the Heddon line up to 1925 and both models today are scarce collectibles. During his tenure at Heddon, Welch obtained seven patents; five for level wind mechanisms, one for an integrated rod and reel, and one for an oil-bearing cover.

The most unusual reels made by Heddon were the 4-15 and 4-18 with a level wind similar to a windshield wiper. Highly coveted by collectors today, these reels were considered unattractive by the anglers of the twenties. Introduced also in the early twenties: the 3-35 model with a life span of four years. The last of the Heddon quality reels was the 3-25, marketed from 1926 to 1931. By the mid-thirties it became impractical to manufacture reels of other than aluminum construction.

Jack Welch left the Heddon firm in 1931 to produce reels on his own. They were mainly tournament models and, though of late antique reel origin, are deemed highly rare collectibles.

Both William Carter and Jack Welch transformed the well-known Heddon lure makers into mass-producers of high quality, outstanding reels.

Two early handmade Heddon reels by Jack Welch. Value: left: $1,200; right: $2,500.

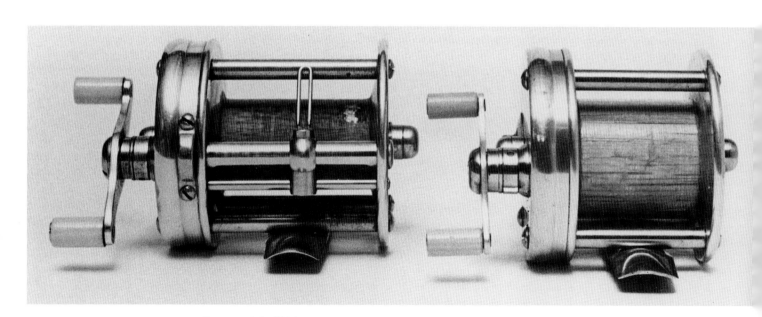

Custom reels by Welch.
Left: Level-wind model. Value: $1,200.
Right: Narrow-spool tournament wood-spool caster (1915 to 1920). Value: $1,500.

Jack Welch, "Dowagiac;" screw drag tensioner. Value: $1,200.

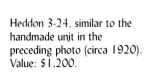

Heddon 3-24, similar to the handmade unit in the preceding photo (circa 1920). Value: $1,200.

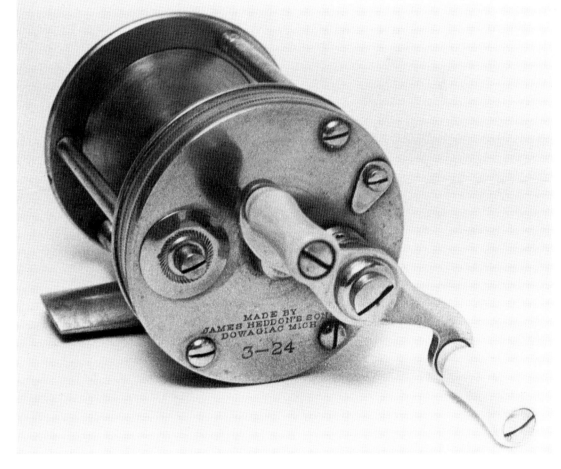

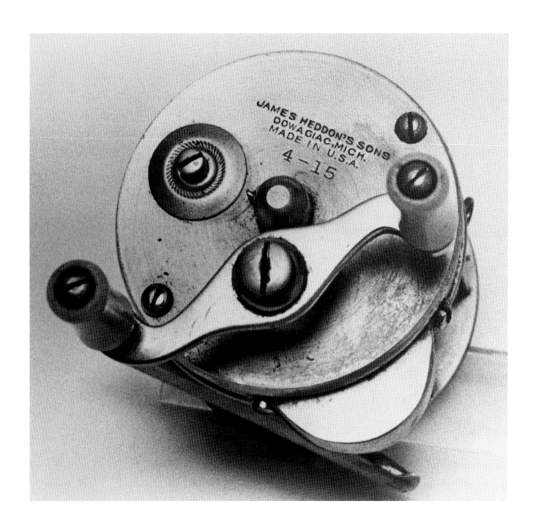

Model 4-15.
Value: $2,500.

Model 4-18. Like the model
4-15, it featured the new
windshield wiper level-wind.
Value: $2,500.

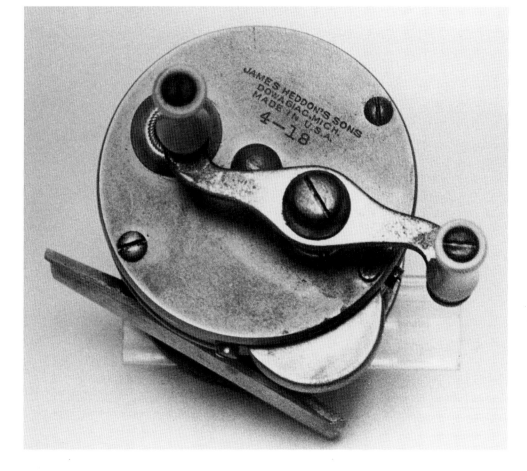

Left: A standard Heddon 3-24. Value: $1,200.
Right: The same model marketed by T.J. Young. Value: $1,400.

Heddon model 330 produced in the early twenties. Value: $800.

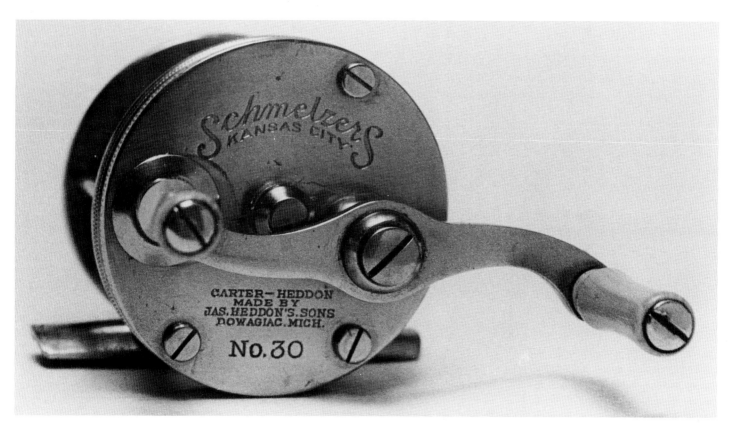

Model 30. Carter-Heddon, marketed by Schmelrers, Kansas City. Value: $3,000.

A model 3-15 styled by Welch. Value: $250.

The model 3-25 sold between 1926 and 1931. Value: $300.

The 3-35 featured a Welch designed oil cap. Value: $300.

A later #40, sold in the 1930s. Value: $1,500.

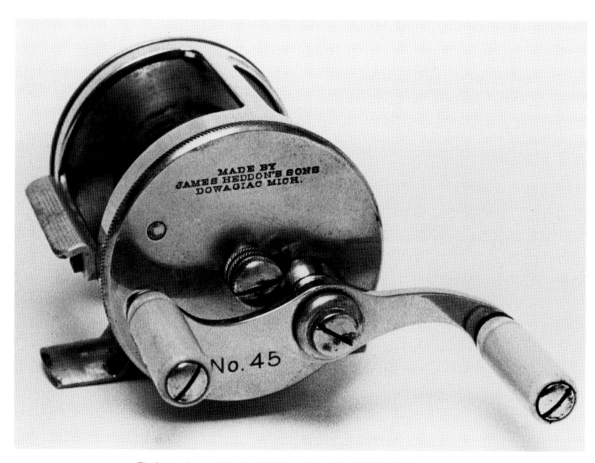

The last reels were like the #45 shown here after Welch left the company
in 1931. This was to be the standard Heddon design. Value: $450.

Ocean City

The firm of Ocean City was incorporated in Philadelphia, Pennsylvania on March 5th of 1923 – its sole purpose, to manufacture and market reels and tackle. In 1939, Ocean City purchased the remarkable assets of Edward Vom Hofe after his unfortunate demise.

The earlier reels were reels produced in the Vom Hofe style; German silver and hard rubber featured in "Ike Walton" surf reels. In the 1920s, and well into the 1950s, Ocean City prevailed in the production of reasonably priced big game as well as conventional tackle reels. Their reels were featured in the Montague and Abby & Imbrie catalogs. A close relationship developed between Montague and Ocean City after the latter company purchased Montague in 1935. On August 1st, 1955, the name of the corporation was officially changed to the "Montague-Ocean City Rod and Reel Co." The largest reels produced in this venture were the "Balboa" series in sizes 12/0 and 10/0. A model with extra-long pillars in size 14/0 was soon to follow in 1938. In the late 1940s, still larger versions of the Balboa were marketed, namely a 16/0 cradle reel.

Ocean City was eventually forced to cease production, edged out by the lower priced Penn "Senator" line in the 1950s. While early Ocean City reels could not emulate the fine craftsmanship of the late Edward Vom Hofe designs, Ocean City was a major contributor to fine, well-priced tackle and their earliest model reels are fine collectibles.

Early Ocean City star drag surfer, circa 1925. Value: $40.

Left: Unmarked reel, most probably by Ocean City,
produced in the early period. Value: $30.
Right: Ocean City free-spool after Vom Hofe. Value: $40.

Ocean City saltwater caster (1930-1940). Value: $40.

Small Ocean City bait caster, sporting a new oval shape. Value: $40.

Ocean City model 1950; windshield wiper level-wind. Value: $30.

Ocean City 2000; small bass-caster; common, no high value. Value: $30.

Otto Zwarg

One of the most notable of the independent reel makers was Otto Zwarg. Known as Florida's master reel maker, Zwarg was born in Berlin, Germany, but migrated to the United States in 1922. He found work with the illustrious Edward Vom Hofe in 1923, grew to admire and love the crafting of reels and soon rose to head of reel production at the Vom Hofe facility. World War II put a damper on Vom Hofe output and Zwarg's tenure ended when the Vom Hofe firm went out of business in 1940.

To survive, Zwarg took a job with the U.S. Government working on the Norden bombsight. He moonlighted on the side repairing Vom Hofe reels and refinishing split bamboo reels.

In 1940, striking out on his own, Zwarg began duplicating some of Vom Hofe's popular reels with Vom Hofe's permission, who stated: "I know of no one so well equipped and qualified to carry on the great tradition of fine, custom built reels." Zwarg moved his family to St. Petersburg, Florida, in 1947 and opened up his business supported by four other stockholders.

Zwarg numbered his reels starting with a letter prefix. The "A" prefix designated reels made in 1946; the "B" prefix identified reels produced in 1947. Early "A" reels are inscribed with his earlier Brooklyn, New York, address; some "B's" have the Brooklyn, and some the newer Florida address. "C" models on up all carry the Florida location. The prefix "M" indicates the year Zwarg died, 1958. It is assumed that reels with an "N" or "O" prefix were made by workers assembling Zwarg's reels after his death. Zwarg built some beautiful reels in Vom Hofe tradition, in which he was schooled, utilizing German silver fittings and hard rubber end caps. Though they are prized by collectors, they do not emanate the charisma attributed to the Vom Hoffe reels. Zwarg's reel output spanned a period of four decades. Some of his reels are featured in the color section of this book.

Penn

Penn was a latecomer, but a strong contender in reel manufacturing, rising to great popularity and is still in business to date, creating bait and big game surf-casting reels. Penn produced reels as far back as 1930, but the Penn Fishing Tackle Manufacturing Co. was officially founded in 1932 by Otto Henze.

The first reel was a model "F" surfcaster, inexpensive, sans star-drag, of nickel-plated brass and bakelite. To allow the reel to free-spool, the handle was pulled to disengage, and pushed back in to engage the retrieval gear. By 1935, the Penn line of reels included eight models from the inexpensive "Newport™" to the most expensive "Coronado™", a star-drag unit of German silver (chrome-plated) with a free spooling clutch.

In 1936, Otto Henze designed the 9/0 "Senator™". Two years later, he masterminded the "Squidder™", an excellent, reasonably priced, surf-casting reel. Soon after its inception, the "Senator" became the exemplary reel of the fishing tackle industry. Price-wise, it forced many reel manufacturers of the period out of the market. After a short hiatus (1942-1945) the company came back, along with a host of other American manufacturers, expanding reel production within the booming post-war economy.

Since Penn is still active in reel and tackle production, earlier models do not raise eyebrows as prime collectibles. They are far from antique desirables, though they are examples of reel production excellence.

The Penn 60. Price made Penn popular. Value: $25.

Langley

Langley, another latecomer, came into existence in 1948, after producing wartime parts. The Langley reels were constructed of high tensile aluminum with stainless steel shafts and a composite spool, which aided in hindering corrosion. Other companies realized the value of lightweight spools and soon followed suit. One of the oldest Langley's is a fly reel, basic and simple as most fly reels. Another identifying Langley characteristic is a crinkle finish on the back plate. The spool was secured by a hex bolt, which also served as the hind piece of the shaft. Other initial Langley models include the R-191-A and R-191-B, both with diameters of three and a quarter inches. The R-192-A and B models were slightly larger in circumference.

The B models featured a line guide as well as a quick release spool. The B model also included a tension adjustment knob. Lightweight perforated spools were another distinctive feature of the Langley's.

Part of the collectible value attributed to the Langley reels stems from the aesthetics of the Langley boxes. Some have "Langley" scripted on the tops, others on the side in unison with the winged logo, which contains the company's origin: San Diego, California. One of the most striking boxes is the 191-A fly reel container in Pea-Green, the only one of its kind amongst the Langley boxes. The logo has a large "L" over a dark circle in conjunction with the Langley winged symbol. Langley produced a number of fine casting and fly reels.

Left: A Langley Shorty with box. Value: $50.
Right: Langley unknown. Value: $30.

Bronson Reel Co.

In the twentieth century, the firms of Shakespeare, Pflueger, and Heddon were firmly entrenched in the reel business with few other large manufacturers save for Penn, which was rapidly encroaching on the field. Another late producer was "Bronson," but their existence was short-lived. They slipped into the field in 1960, but closed shop in 1967. Though not "oldies," some of the Bronson's are considered "goodies" with their renowned "Invader 26" fetching $350.00 to $400.00 on current E-Bay auctions; a prime price for an average collectible reel.

The "Invader" was an aluminum reel with a push-button free-spool release, star-drag, and non-reversing crank. It was distinctively styled, sporting an oval shape, attractive with red and black coloring and chrome trim. It utilized nylon drive and pinion gears similar to later Shakespeare reels. A late model of the "Invader 26" was sold with a Bronson logo, but also marketed with J.A. Coxe labels. Wards also marketed a similar Bronson piece labeled "Wards Hawthorne".

Early Bronson Mercury. Value: $30.

Left to Right: Bronson #1100 casting reel (Veteran); Bronson #4200 (Altoona); Bronson #4700 (Blackstone). Values: $25 each.

Closing this chapter are photos of a few other reels that were popularized in the twentieth century.

Expert 20, early 1920s. Value: $200.

J.A. Coxe early twentieth century. Value: $500.

Early twentieth century reels; known names; origin unknown. Value: left: $200; right: $150.

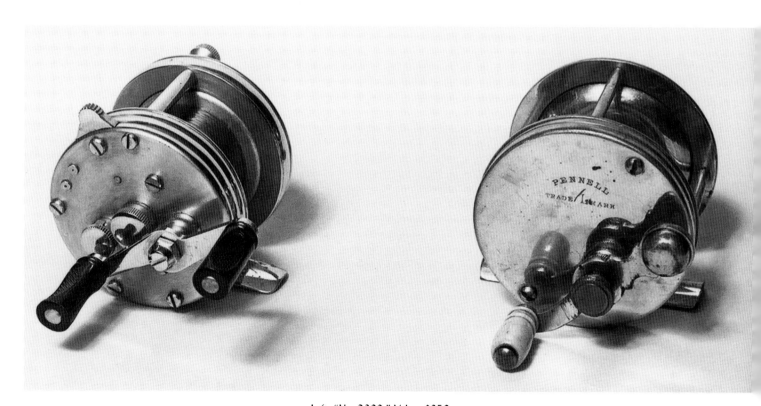

Left: "Abu 2300." Value: $350.
Right: "Pennell." Value: $50.

Record Sport 2100, Swedish origin. Value: $350.

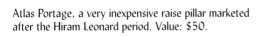

Atlas Portage, a very inexpensive raise pillar marketed after the Hiram Leonard period. Value: $50.

Abbey and Imbrie, produced by Meisselbach, early part of the twentieth century. Value: $160.

Perez No. 1 reel. Value: $275.

Chapter VI
Fly Reels

Fly reels are the simplest of reels; very basic, the precursor of reels as we know them today. The first fly reel consisted of its frame, spool, and retrieving handle.

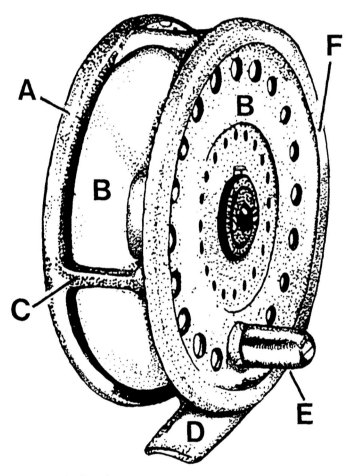

Anatomy of a fly reel.
A. Backplate
B. Spool
C. Pillar
D. Foot
E. Handle
F. Faceplate

Through innovation and evolution, we have today three types: single action, multiplying gear action, and automatic retrieve. Each has its own school of angling supporters.

In a single action fly reel the diameter of the spool combined with the simplest gear ratio (1:1) translates into one complete turn of line pulled in with each full revolution of the handle. To atone for loss of retrieval speed, better single action reels rely on narrow spools with large diameters for quicker recovery. A drag mechanism may be incorporated to add tension or generate slack when required.

Multiplier reels are not as crucial or desirable amongst fly fishers; virtually all marketed to date have not evolved into favorable designs. The most popular multipliers contain 2:1 retrieval ratios.

Automatic fly reels provide mechanical line retrieval, utilizing spring-loaded mechanisms usually activated by index finger pressure release. The drawback to automatic reels is excessive weight, which tends to inhibit rod balance and control when lines are cast.

The fly reel had its origin in Great Britain, sometime around the 1830s. A new narrow brass spooled reel was produced in Birmingham, England, hence referred to as the Birmingham reel. It is believed that the first commercial Birmingham reel was produced in the mid-1800s. Early reels used in America were imported from England, although it appears that some reels were created on our home grounds in Kentucky and New York as early as the 1820s. As American maker adapted early English reels, one of the developments resulted in the New York multiplying reel design. This reel's intent was for use in striped bass fishing off the Atlantic Coast, but soon gravitated toward fly-fishing for salmon. These early New York reels featured a wood or bone knob at one end of the crank, and a ball shaped brass counterweight at the other extreme end of the crank. Later versions were fabricated in German silver and some reel smiths began styling S-shaped cranks also counterbalanced typical of reel examples by J.C. Conroy & Co.

Some experimentation with fly reel side mounting was seen in the late 1870s by such reel smiths as Billinghurst, Meisselbach, Clinton, and Fowler. The Fowler Gem was the first fly reel utilizing hard rubber in its constructional makeup. Patented in 1872, the 2 3/4, one and a half ounce model was very fragile and very few exist today: less than a dozen. In the late nineteenth century, small multiplying reels were in favor and they were suitable for either light bait casting or fly-casting. J.C. Conroy, William Mills, B.F. Meek, and the Vom Hofe's produced many multipliers.

Fly Reel Manufacturers

Hiram Leonard – The Raised Pillar Concept

Leonard was a throwback to the 1870s, when he first began fabricating reels. His tackle continued to sell well into the first decade of the twentieth century. Leonard was also considered by high-ranking experts to be the finest rod craftsman of his time, as well as a leading gunsmith. Originally from Bangor, Maine, Leonard moved to reestablish his tackle operation in Central Valley, New York, in 1881.

Leonard's famed raised pillar reel was originally conceived by Francis J. Philbrook in 1877; but, rights to the design were assigned to Leonard at the patent's inception. In the late 1890s, the production of raised pillar reels was transferred to the shop of Julius Vom Hofe. Vom Hofe, in addition, also produced spinoffs of the Leonard raised pillar design, with Leonard's benediction. Vom Hofe continued to fabricate Leonard-style reels up to the beginning of the Second World War.

The Leonard reel became very popular with anglers because of its fortified construction and aesthetic excellence. It is the earliest reel to feature protective rims around the spool, another design element widely copied for years to come.

Hiram Leonard raised pillar reel – 1896. Value: $1,500.

Early Julius Vom Hofe raised pillar. Value: $400.

Other Leonard reels can be seen in our color section.

Other companies also specialized in raised pillar reels, but usually of lesser quality. The Andrew B. Hendryx Co. of New Haven, Connecticut, made some nickel-plated brass renditions, starting in 1888. Raised pillar single-action Hendryx reels were made in differing styles and finishes, all of stamped steel, and were introduced as early as 1890 in quantity. They continued to be offered, sustaining minor changes up to the 1920s, when they were bought out by Winchester Arms.

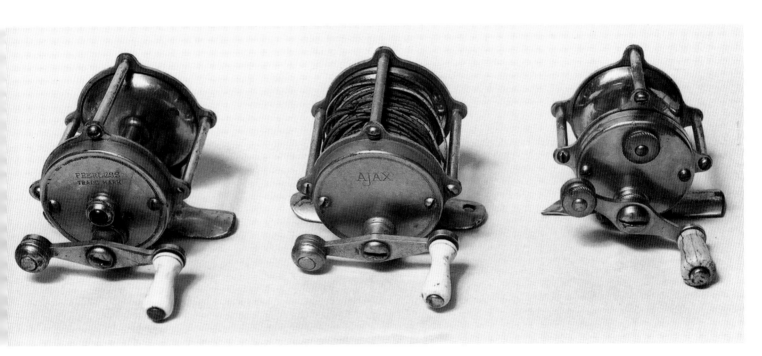

Left: Peerless. Value: $40.
Center: Ajax. Value: $30.
Right: U.K. cheap punched, raised pillar reels. Value: $40.

The following are some photos of critical reels of the first quarter of the twentieth century.

Left: Rueben Heaton, Birmingham trout reel; 1890. Value: $200.
Right: Unknown. Value: $200.

Left: Rogan Ballyshannon. Value: $350.
Center: Pflueger Progress. Value: $75.
Right: Unknown. Value: $200.

Left: David Slater, 1900. Value: $150.
Right: No name, but attributed to David Slater. Value: $150.

Meisselbach Rainbow. Value: $25.

Early Pflueger Medalist, 1900-1920. Value: $30.

Hardy Bros. Ltd.

Hardy fly reels are the epitome of fly reel crafting excellence and quality. To this day, they are the finest fly reels available. The firm is of British origin, founded in 1872 by William Hardy. Since its inception, the Hardy name has been synonymous with state of the art reel craftsmanship.

In 1873, William was joined by his brother John James and the duo partook in a joint venture gunsmithing and knife crafting. The siblings soon took a fancy to fishing tackle and the Hardy fly reel was born.

Aside from reels, the Hardy boys produced fine rods, the finest of greenheart wood, then graduating to split bamboo, a medium more conducive to fly reel construction. Soon the reel business superceded all their other endeavors, their reputation flourished, and the Hardy reels were desired throughout the world.

The Hardys produced a vast array of reels, but the Hardy "Perfect™" is the most acclaimed and very likely the finest reel style the brothers produced. The all-brass original "Perfect" was the first design to emanate from the machine shop. It is much sought after by collectors, considered the most valuable and highest priced of all Hardy issue. It was first fabricated in 1890, a machining tour-de-force as its spool rotated on ball bearings, an innovation initiated by a third brother who joined the fold in the same year.

The earliest Hardy reels were fashioned totally from brass, but in the late 1890s an aluminum alloy was introduced. This alloy was used for the spools and frames, but the faceplates retained their brass facade.

Each Hardy employee constructed a reel from beginning to end, by hand, by himself. Names and numbers were stamped on each reel and usually the assembler's initials. In time, the brass-faced "Perfect" superceded the all-brass "Perfect". In some cases the brass faceplate was bronzed, giving it a black-gray finish. A few were given silver-bronze coatings to resist tarnishing.

Around 1900, the narrow drum Perfect reels were issued using the same alloy framing and still a brass face. These early "Rod in Hand™" stamped models are rare, since they were in production for a mere five years. Early Hardy models sported ivory or elk horn handles, but these natural substances were later replaced by "Ivorine," a synthetic material less prone to brittleness and cracking. Wide drum Hardy models were also offered in circumferences up to five inches wide, which were predominately salmon reels.

Though the Hardy establishment is still faring well today, it is mainly producing modern state of the art renderings of their original Hardy concept. The famous Hardy collectible, the Hardy "Perfect", went out of production in 1994. Hardy Bros. Ltd. is one of the few specialized reel manufacturers of today dating back to the nineteenth century.

Early Hardy Perfect, 1900. Value: $300.

Hardy Perfect with Agate guide. Value: $400.

Hardy "Uniqua." Value with box: $250.

Left: Hardy "J.W. Young" Perfect Featherlite. Value: $300.
Right: Hardy "Exchequer." Value: $350.

Rear view of reels in the previous photo.

Charles F. Orvis

Studying the English influence, Orvis patented his famed Trout reel, which was a cross section of ideas. This reel enjoyed much commercial success after patenting on May 12, 1874.

Sold directly from Orvis in Manchester, Vermont, the Trout reel was also marketed through an expansive dealer network. This reel was even exported to England where it gained favor because of its narrow spool and highly perforated face and rear plate.

Left: Hardy. Value: $150.
Right: Orvis Madison. Value: $100.

Two unknown turntable casters, circa 1940. Values: $200 each.

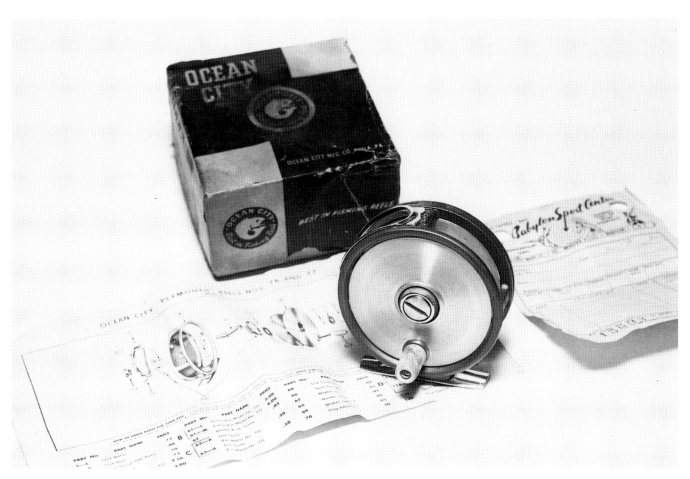

Ocean City Plymouth. Value: $30.

Fin-Nor Wedding Cake reels. Values: $1,150.

Automatic Fly Reels

Though considered modern, automatics date back to Loomis, who pulled the first patent and is mentioned earlier in this book. Martin automatic was a popular contender in the automatic reel race back in 1892 when they also received a patent for their design. To this day, Martin remains the largest manufacturer of automatic reels.

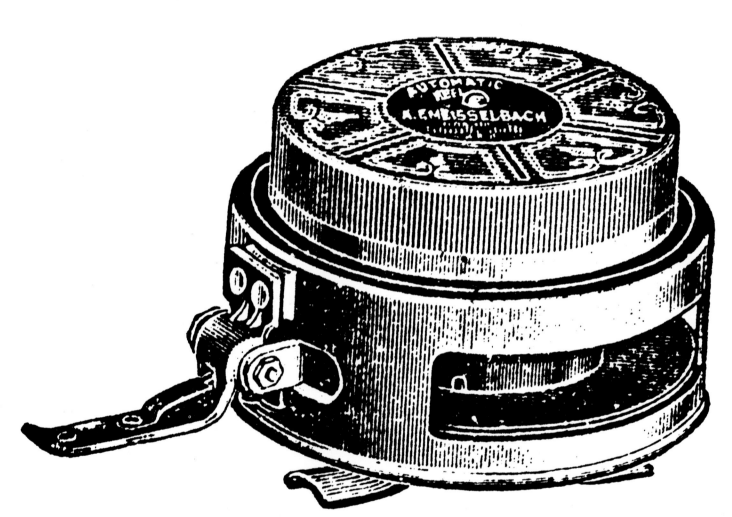

MEISSELBACH
Automatic Reel

Meisselbach Auto reel. Value: $60.

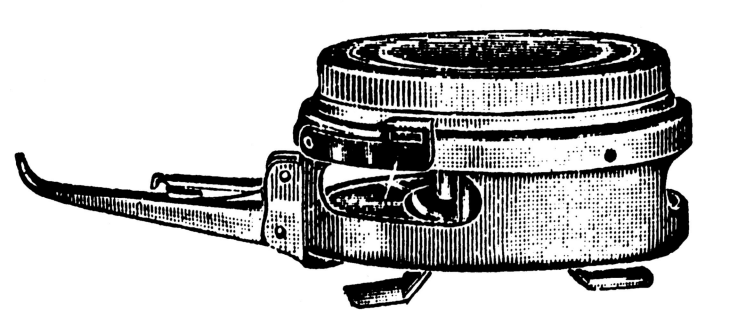

MARTIN AUTOMATIC

Martin Automatic. Value: $35.

Pflueger Superex; Nov. 19, 1907 patent. Value: $30.

Martin presentation, engraved piece. Value: $100.

Shakespeare Automatic fly reel. "Silent Automatic." Value: $25.

Salmon Reels

Salmon reels are in a class by themselves; usually larger than trout and freshwater fly reels. They must also be stronger with bulkier gears to handle large, hard fighting salmon. Some anglers feel that the added weight and bulk of the salmon reel acts as a counterweight, enabling fishermen with extra long rods to better balance the stick when fighting a large fish.

The most notable salmon fly reel retailers of the mid-nineteenth to the twentieth century were Thomas J. Conroy and Hiram Leonard. Other craftsmen were also producing salmon reels in the U.S., but on a lower output level. Edward Vom Hofe was also instrumental in creating the finest salmon reels, which are in use to this day, but not by collectors who favor them as prime collectable pieces. In 1926, Vom Hofe offered the "Griswold" with an offset handle, which did not make it too popular with salmon fishers as it impeded orderly line retrieval. The "Tobique" issued shortly after was a far more successful center cranking, multiplying reel. Thumb control was essential in salmon reels, but painstaking in terms of drag control. In 1878, Vom Hofe began employing a crown-ratchet gear to raise or lower the height of leather-topped spring clutch, which served as a form of positive drag control.

Today, salmon reels larger than 4/0 are virtually obsolete, save for some large, high capacity saltwater reels.

Fly Reel Values

Brand	Type / Model	Value
Abbey & Imbrie	25 yd	$65.00
Abbey & Imbrie	Hardy look-alike	$100.00
Abel	#5, 3-inch Black	$290.00
Abel	#5, Adjustable Drag Nylon Case	$295.00
Abel	#0, 2 3/4-inch, Black	$240.00
Abel	#1, 3 1/4-inch, Black	$325.00
Abel	#5 Bluewater	$1,000.00
Abel	TR-1 Black	$250.00
Abel	TR-2 Gold Frame	$335.00
Abel	TR-3 Black	$275.00
Abercrombie & Fitch	Hardy Featherweight	$120.00
Abercrombie & Fitch	Hardy Flyweight	$145.00
Abercrombie & Fitch	Yellowstone	$25.00
L. Ackerman	#8234	$50.00
Allcock	Aerial	$125.00
Allcock	Aerial 3 1/2"	$425.00
Allcock	Marvel 3 3/4"	$50.00
Allcock	Marvel 4	$95.00
Allcock	Conquest	$105.00
S. Allcock & Co.	Gilmour 3 1/8"	$85.00
S. Allcock & Co.	3" by J.W. Young	$95.00
Ambassadeur (Sweden)	3" Trout	$80.00
R. Anderson & Sons	Brass Salmon 4 1/4"	$130.00
Angler	Rainbow – Greg Spool	$15.00
A.P.I.	Black 2x Spool	$495.00
A.P.I.	Black 3 3/4" Anti-Reverse	$525.00
A.P.I.	Special Limited Ed. (only 100 made)	$400.00
A.P.I.	Spring Creek with pouch	$260.00
Appleton & Bassett	Fly, 2 1/4"	$165.00
Arnold Bivens	Green, Wide Spool	$20.00
Arnold Products	Allison, 4" Adj. Drag	$195.00
Ath	F3, Lake Taupo	$275.00
Ath	Rio Orbigo, 3 1/2"	$325.00

Brand	Type / Model	Value
L.L. Bean	#10	$30.00
L.L. Bean	#77	$25.00
Berkley	#510	$15.00
Pat Billinghurst	Model I, 1859 3 1/2"	$1,600.00
Pat Billinghurst	Birdcage 1859	$12,000.00
Pat Billinghurst	Model II – 3"	$700.00
Pat Billinghurst	Brass Birdgage	$1,540.00
Wm. Billinghurst	1859 Patent	$795.00
Bivans	Green, 3 3/4 3 pos. Drag	$25.00
Blackhawk	Autofly	$15.00
Bogdan	Black 3 1/4" Goldcase	$1,100.00
Bogdan	0 Salmon Multiplier	$1,700.00
Bogdan	00 Multiplier 3 1/2"	$1,650.00
Bogdan	300m Salmon, 3 3/4"	$1,850.00
Bogdan	Baby Trout	$1,550.00
Bogdan	300 Salmon Multiplier	$1,295.00
Bogdan	Trout, 3 1/4" "S" Handle	$1,150.00
Bogdan	Steelhead 3 1/4"	$1,500.00
Bogdan	Wide Trout, 3 1/4"	$1,450.00
S.E. Bogdan	Black Narrow Trout 3 1/4"	$1,500.00
S.E. Bogdan	Small Narrow Trout, 2 3/4" Gold	$1,500.00
Brass	1 3/4" with Stop Latch	$275.00
Brass	Ball Handle, 2 1/8" Rare	$220.00
Brass	Ball Handle 3"	$150.00
Brass	Small, Machined Brass	$120.00
Brass	40-yd., Counterbalanced	$60.00
Brass	Tiny 25-yd. Collar Fitted	$120.00
Brass	Primitive, Ball Handle	$220.00
Brass	Skeleton Fly / Black Enamel	$10.00
Duncan Briggs	#2	$12.00
Bristol-Horton	#65 Anodized 3 1/2"	$30.00
Bristol-Horton	#65 Black Enamel 3 1/2"	$25.00
Bronson	#360 Royal	$25.00
Bronson	#380 Multi-Royal	$30.00
Bronson	#390 Royal Matic	$20.00
Bronson	#560 Royal, 3 3/8"	$25.00
J.A. Burkholder	#PKT Trout	$75.00
Herb Butler	Standard Fly	$30.00
Carlton	Ideal	$65.00
Carlton Mfg. Co.	Fly-Standard	$45.00
Conroy	#5 (tiny) Silver	$250.00
J.C. Conroy, N.Y.	Nickle Silver	$495.00
Thomas J. Conroy	#3, Nickle Silver	$375.00
Thomas J. Conroy	JVH Pat. 1989	$495.00
Cortland	3 1/4"	$12.00
Cortland	Pro Crest 3 1/2"	$35.00
Cozzone	60-yd. 2 1/4"	$225.00
Cozzone	Midge Fly	$245.00
Cozzone	80-yd.	$275.00
L.M. Dickson	Maginot	$30.00
Briggs Duncan	Fixed Check, 3 3/8"	$40.00
Briggs Duncan	Black, Constant Check	$15.00
Briggs Duncan	#2	$12.00
Edwards	#30, 2 7/8"	$15.00
Edwards	#40, 3 3/4"	$10.00
Edwards	#40, Aluminum	$20.00
Farlow	Brass Guard, 2 5/8"	$280.00
Farlow	Cobra 3 1/2"	$100.00
Farlow	Python, Adj. Drag	$100.00
Farlow	Python, 4" Salmon	$100.00
Farlow	Sapphire 3 1/8"	$50.00
Harrison Felton	Archangel, 4 1/4"	$1,200.00
Harrison Felton	Little Wing II, 3 5/8" (only 5 manufactured)	$1,100.00
Fenwick	Class 4, 3 1/4" Gold, Black	$350.00
Fenwick	Class 4, Gold, Aluminum, Black	$450.00
Fenwick	Class 6, Trout 3 1/2"	$150.00
Feurer Bros.	Gold Seal, 3 3/4"	$175.00

Brand	Type / Model	Value	Brand	Type / Model	Value
Fin-Nor	#1, 3" Bag & Box	$350.00	Hardy	Silex #2, 4"	$250.00
Fin-Nor	#1, Trout Reel with Pouch	$350.00	Hardy	Silex Major	$350.00
Fin-Nor	#1, Tycoon	$900.00	Hardy	Sovereign, Gold; Adj. Drag, 2 3/4"	$275.00
Fin-Nor	#2, Early Wedding Cake	$700.00	Hardy	Special Perfect, 2 1/4"	$500.00
Fin-Nor	#3, Anti-Reverse 3 3/4"	$295.00	Hardy	St. Aiden, 3 3/4"	$200.00
Fin-Nor	#3, Wedding Cake 4"	$850.00	Hardy	St. Aiden Salmon, 3 3/4"	$150.00
Fin-Nor	#1, 3" Post Wedding Cake	$320.00	Hardy	St. Andrews, 4 1/8"	$200.00
Fin-Nor	#2, 3 1/8" Post Wedding Cake	$320.00	Hardy	St. George, 2 9/16", Aluminum	$550.00
Fin-Nor	#3 Second Model, 3 5/8"	$325.00	Hardy	St. George, Enamel Finish, 3"	$300.00
Fin-Nor	#3, Wedding Cake	$725.00	Hardy	St. George, White Agate, 3"	$600.00
Fin-Nor	Wedding Cake, 4" Garwood	$1,150.00	Hardy	St. George Jr., Enamel, 2 9/16"	$400.00
Finlay-Falkirk	Trout Reel, 3 1/4" Aluminum	$170.00	Hardy	St. George, Jr., White Agate, 2 9/16"	$700.00
Ashbourne-Foster	All Brass Birmingham Type	$80.00	Hardy	St. John, 3 7/8"	$165.00
Four Brothers	Delight 40-yd.	$155.00	Hardy	St. John, Brass Ribbed Foot, 3 7/8"	$120.00
Four Brothers	Delight 60-yd.	$120.00	Hardy	St. John, Aluminum Foot, 3 7/8"	$125.00
Gayle	#2, Simplicity	$25.00	Hardy	St. John, Salmon, Late	$100.00
Gayle	#6, Simplicity	$25.00	Hardy	Sunbeam, 2 3/4"	$150.00
Hardy	Birmingham, 2 3/8" Brass	$450.00	Hardy	Sunbeam, Wire Line Guide, 3"	$250.00
Hardy	Bougle, 3 1/4"	$1,750.00	Hardy	Super Silex, 3 3/4"	$450.00
Hardy	Altex #1 Mark V	$150.00	Hardy	Davy, Brass Foot, 3 1/2"	$2,500.00
Hardy	Altex #2 Mark III	$130.00	Hardy	Elarex, Level Wind	$250.00
Hardy	Altex #3 Mark V	$150.00	Hardy	Hydra, Single Pawl	$50.00
Hardy	Birmingham 2 3/8" Brass	$450.00	Hardy	Uniqua, 2 5/8"	$200.00
Hardy	Bougle, 3 1/4"	$1,750.00	Hardy	Uniqua, 2 7/8"	$120.00
Hardy	Cascapedia 7 Position Drag	$5,900.00	Hardy	Uniqua, 3 1/8"	$125.00
Hardy	Cascapedia, Black Anodized	$3,900.00	Hardy	Uniqua, 3 3/8"	$140.00
Hardy	Featherweight, 2 3/4"	$160.00	Hardy	Uniqua, 3 5/8"	$125.00
Hardy	Flyweight 2 1/2"	$100.00	Hardy	Uniqua, Von Lengerke & Detmold, 3 1/2"	$110.00
Hardy	Gem 3 1/4"	$180.00			
Hardy	Golden Prince 4 1/4"	$300.00	Hardy	Uniqua, "OK" 9, 3 1/8"	$125.00
Hardy	Hercules (early), 2 1/2"	$1,000.00	Hardy	Uniqua Salmon, 3 3/4"	$300.00
Hardy	Hercules Trout, Brass, 2 1/2"	$1,000.00	Hardy	Viscount #130	$100.00
Hardy	Husky, 3 1/4"	$125.00	Hardy	Viscount #150	$100.00
Hardy	Husky Salmon, 3 3/8"	$200.00	Hardy	Zenith, 3 1/4"	$195.00
Hardy	Husky Salmon, Silent Drag	$170.00	Hardy	Zenith, 3 3/8"	$170.00
Hardy	Lightweight, 3 1/8"	$100.00	Harris Reel	Gloversville, N.Y.	$350.00
Hardy	Longstone, 4 1/2"	$200.00	Hart	Marquesa (1970)	$200.00
Hardy	LRH	$120.00	Hart	Limpqua Marquesa	$250.00
Hardy	LRH Early Model	$250.00	Hart	Limpqua Salmon	$300.00
Hardy	LRH Lightweight, 3 3/16"	$200.00	Hart Reel Co.	Marquesa, Black & Chrome (1978), 3 3/4"	$625.00
Hardy	Marquis #10, 3 7/8"	$120.00			
Hardy	Marquis #5, 3"	$125.00	Haskell	2 3/4"	$500.00
Hardy	Marquis #6, 3 1/4"	$125.00	Haskell	Narrow Spool, 3 3/8"	$450.00
Hardy	Marquis #7	$100.00	Heddon	#125 Imperial, 3 1/4"	$150.00
Hardy	Marquis #8, 3 5/8"	$100.00	Heddon	#340, 3 3/4"	$35.00
Hardy	Marquis Salmon #1, 3 7/8"	$120.00	Heddon	#37, Auto Fly	$25.00
Hardy	Marquis Salmon #2, 4 1/8"	$125.00	Heddon	#5, Auto Fly	$80.00
Hardy	Perfect, 2 3/4" Wide Drum (1905)	$750.00	Heddon	#57, Auto Fly, Bronze	$30.00
Hardy	Perfect, Brass Face, 2 5/8"	$1,200.00	Horrocks-Ibbotson	#1106	$20.00
Hardy	Perfect, Black, 2 7/8"	$180.00	Horrocks-Ibbotson	#1107 Rainbow	(*Value?)
Hardy	Perfect, Agate, 2 7/8"	$600.00	Horrocks-Ibbotson	Utica Auto Fly	$10.00
Hardy	Perfect, 3 1/8", Extra Spool, Agate	$150.00	Horrocks-Ibbotson	Vernley Trout	$35.00
Hardy	Perfect, Narrow Drum (1905)	$850.00	Horton-Meek	#54, 2 15/16"	$135.00
Hardy	Perfect, Brass Face Drum, 3 3/4"	$1,500.00	Horton-Meek	#55, 3 1/8"	$150.00
Hardy	Perfect, Enamel Finish, 3 5/8"	$145.00	Horton-Meek	#56, 3 3/8"	$125.00
Hardy	Perfect, Maroon	$230.00	Ideal	#2	$75.00
Hardy	Perfect Narrow Drum (1922), 3 3/8"	$395.00	Langley	Riffle, 3 1/4"	$35.00
Hardy	Perfect, Rare Red Agate, 3 3/8"	$1,100.00	Lawson	#1 Laurentian	$15.00
Hardy	Perfect, White Ceramic Line Guide, 3 5/8"	$185.00	Lawson Machine Works	#2 Laurentian, Black	$20.00
Hardy	Perfect, Red Ceramic Line Guide, 3 3/8"	$175.00	Leonard	Light Salmon, 3 5/8"	$600.00
Hardy	Perfect, Ebonite Knob, 3 5/8"	$280.00	Leonard	Fairy Trout	$1,100.00
Hardy	Perfect, Salmon, Wide Spool, 3 1/2"	$495.00	Leonard-Mills	"Mills" Name, 2 3/4"	$695.00
Hardy	Prince, 3"	$170.00	Leonard-Mills	#48, 3 3/4"	$495.00
Hardy	Princess, 3 1/2"	$125.00	Leonard-Mills	#50, 3 1/8"	$900.00
Hardy	Scientific Angler, 4" Extra Spool	$150.00	Leonard-Mills	Midge, 2 3/8"	$1,200.00
Hardy	Scientific Angler, Marquis Copy, 3"	$175.00	Leonard-Mills	Midge Click	$750.00
Hardy	Scientific Angler, Adj. Drag, 3"	$150.00	Leonard-Mills	Salmon, 4 1/4"	$600.00

Brand	Type / Model	Value	Brand	Type / Model	Value
Leonard-Mills	Trout Reel by Julius Vom Hofe	$950.00	Peerless	#2 Trout, 3 1/4"	$350.00
H.L. Leonard	Bi-Metal, Brass, 2 3/8"	$1,400.00	Peerless	#2A, 3 1/4"	$450.00
H.L. Leonard	#191813 Patent, 2 5/8"	$900.00	Peerless	#3, 3 1/4"	$450.00
H.L. Leonard	Salmon, 4 1/4"	$500.00	Peerless	#3A, 3 1/4"	$430.00
H.L. Leonard	Click Reel-Trout, 2 1/8"	$1,700.00	Peerless	#5, 3 1/4"	$450.00
Leonard Mills & Son	Aluminum Spool, 3 3/4"	$500.00	Peerless	#5 Salmon	$450.00
Martin	Auto Fly (1923) Silver	$100.00	Peerless	#6, 3 1/2"	$600.00
Martin	Auto Fly (Black)	$15.00	Perrine	#30 Free Stripping	$25.00
Martin	#72 Boxed	$50.00	Perrine	#50 Automatic	$15.00
Martin	#63, 3"	$25.00	Perrine	#50 Free Stripping	$25.00
Martin	#77W, 3 1/4"	$35.00	Pflueger	#1492 Medalist, 2 7/8"	$45.00
Martin	Miracle Matic #500 Auto	$20.00	Pflueger	#1492 Medalist Double Pawl (1930)	$100.00
Martin	Special Presentation Auto	$400.00	Pflueger	#1494 Medalist (early)	$75.00
Meek	#55, Black, 3 1/8"	$70.00	Pflueger	#1498 Medalist, 3 1/2"	$40.00
Meek	#56, 3 1/4"	$100.00	Pflueger	#1496-1/2 Medalist (early)	$100.00
Meisselbach	#17 Partly Plated	$20.00	Pflueger	#1496 Medalist	$30.00
Meisselbach	#17 Expert, 1896 Patent	$60.00	Pflueger	#1498 Medalist	$35.00
Meisselbach	#19 Expert, 2 1/2"	$70.00	Pflueger	#1554 Trout	$35.00
Meisselbach	#19 Expert, Nickel Plated Brass	$75.00	Pflueger	#1554 Salmon, Trout	$20.00
Meisselbach	#19 Expert (1886) Mini Fly Reel	$60.00	Pflueger	#1558 Salmon, Trout, 5 1/2"	$35.00-50.00
Meisselbach	#250 Featherlite	$50.00	Pflueger	#1558 Large Trolling Fly	$25.00
Meisselbach	#260 Featherlite (1904 Patent)	$50.00	Pflueger	#1592 First Model; Rare	$175.00
Meisselbach	#260 Featherlite, Blue Brass	$40.00	Pflueger	#1595 RC Medalist	$30.00
Meisselbach	#280 Featherlite	$50.00	Pflueger	#1774 Progress, 2 7/8"	$25.00
Meisselbach	#290 Featherlite, 1904 Patent, 3"	$60.00	Pflueger	#264 Hawkeye, 2 1/2"	$225.00
Meisselbach	#370 Airex	$65.00	Pflueger	Golden West, 60-yd.	$200.00
Meisselbach	#372 Simploreel	$50.00	Pflueger	Golden West, 80-yd.	$225.00
Meisselbach	Automatic	$35.00	Pflueger	Hawkeye, 60-yd., 2 1/2"	$200.00
Meisselbach	Aluminum Auto, 1914 Patent	$60.00	Pflueger	Hawkeye, 80-yd.	$175.00
Meisselbach	Amateur, 2 1/4"	$50.00	Pflueger	Progress, 60-yd.	$65.00
Wm. Mills	Dry Fly Salmon, 3 1/8"	$600.00	Pflueger	Progress Bulldog, 80-yd.	$50.00
Wm. Mills	Fairy Trout, Vom Hofe	$300.00	Portage	Seminole, 2 3/4"	$50.00
Wm. Mills & Son	Julius Vom Hofe 1896 Patent, 2 1/4"	$100.00	Portage	Seminole, 60-yd.	$60.00
Wm. Mills & Son	Kennett Reel 1920, 3"	$250.00	Precisionbilt	Mosquito, 3"	$50.00
Millward	Flymaster, 3 1/2"	$50.00	Precisionbilt	Silver Moth	$75.00
Millward	Flycraft, 3 1/2"	$80.00	Carlton Rochester	Automatic, 1889-1903 Pat.	$40.00
Montgomery Ward	Sport King, Black, 3"	$25.00	Rome	2 in 1 Automatic (1907 Pat.)	$130.00
Montgomery Ward	#60-6414 Hawthorne, 3 1/4"	$40.00	Ross	#30310 Trout, 3 3/8"	$85.00
North Fork	Trout Fly, 2 7/8"	$170.00	Ross	#3.5, 3 7/16"	$125.00
Ocean City	#36, Black, 3 1/2"	$20.00	Ross	Cimmaron C-3, 3 1/2"	$100.00
Ocean City	#36, Black Enamel, 3 3/8"	$15.00	Ross	Gunnison G-2, 3 1/4"	$220.00
Ocean City	#90 Automatic	$20.00	Ross Reels	Heritage, 2 7/8"	$1,400.00
Ocean City	Viscoy, 3"	$20.00	Ross, Etna, Ca.	#53 Black, 3 5/8"	$140.00
Ocean City	Brass & Aluminum, 3"	$120.00	Scientific Angler	#1112 System 3	$600.00
Orvis	1874 Model, 2 7/8"	$600.00	Scientific Angler	Model 12/13	$185.00
Orvis	Batten Kill, 2 3/4"	$70.00	Scientific Angler	Sys. 11 by Hardy, 4"	$150.00
Orvis	Batten Kill, with Case	$90.00	Scientific Angler	Sys. 5 by Hardy, 3"	$150.00
Orvis	Batten Kill, 3 1/4"	$60.00	Scientific Angler	Model 45L	$90.00
Orvis	Batten Kill, Mark III, 3 1/2"	$85.00	Scientific Angler	Sys. 4	$90.00
Orvis	Batten Kill, Mark IV	$100.00	Scientific Angler	Sys. 4 by Hardy	$125.00
Orvis	Batten Kill, Mark V, 3 1/2"	$100.00	Scientific Angler	Sys. 6 by Hardy, 3 1/4"	$50.00
Orvis	CFO 123, 2 7/8"	$120.00	Scientific Angler	Sys. 8, 3 5/8"	$70.00
Orvis	CFO II	$100.00	Scientific Angler	Sys. 8 by Hardy	$120.00
Orvis	CFO III, 3"	$120.00	Scientific Angler	Sys. I, 3 1/2"	$45.00
Orvis	CFO IV, 3 1/4"	$90.00	Scientific Angler	Sys. II, 3 1/2"	$135.00
Orvis	CFO Trout, 3"	$750.00	Scientific Angler	Sys. II, 3 3/4"	$125.00
Orvis	CFO Trout, 2"	$195.00	Shakespeare	#1821 Auto	$10.00
Orvis	Commemorative 1874, 2 7/8"	$380.00	Shakespeare	#1821 OK Auto	$10.00
Orvis	DXR, 3 1/8"	$175.00	Shakespeare	#1821 Model D Auto (horizontal)	$10.00
Orvis	Green Mountain II, 3 3/8"	$75.00	Shakespeare	#1822 Wondereel Auto	$25.00
Orvis	Presentation EXR II, 3"	$75.00	Shakespeare	#1824 Free Strip Auto	$25.00
Orvis	Presentation EXR III	$125.00	Shakespeare	#1835 Tru Art Auto	$25.00
Orvis	Presentation EXR, IV, 3 1/2"	$165.00	Shakespeare	#1837 Automatic	$20.00
Orvis	Presentation EXR V, 3 3/4"	$150.00	Shakespeare	#1837 Silent	$25.00
Orvis	SSS 11/12, 4" Multiplier	$335.00	Shakespeare	#1864 Au-Sable	$25.00
Billy Plate	Salmon, Black, Suede Case	$275.00	Shakespeare	#1864 Russell Fixed Click, 3"	$25.00
Peerless	#1, 2 3/4"	$320.00	Shakespeare	#1895 Russell, 3 1/2"	$15.00
Peerless	#1 1/2, 3"	$430.00	Shakespeare	#1896 Russell	$40.00

Brand	Type / Model	Value	Brand	Type / Model	Value
Shakespeare	#1900 Steelhead (1936)	$85.00	Walker	#300, Multiplier	$1,000.00
Shakespeare	#2531, 3 5/8"	$30.00	Walker	TR-1	$1,300.00
Shakespeare	#7594 Purist, 3 1/4"	$25.00	Walker	TR-2	$1,000.00
Shakespeare	Alpha	$25.00	Walker	TR-3, 3 1/8"	$900.00
Ogden Smith	Aluminum-Brass, 3"	$125.00	Walker	TR-3 Trout, 3 1/8"	$1,000.00
Ogden Smith	Brass, Gun Metal, 4 1/2"	$350.00	A.L. Walker	#200 Salmon	$1,300.00
Ogden Smith	Flyos, 3"	$70.00	A.L. Walker	#300 Salmon	$975.00
South Bend	#1100 Reno	$15.00	Arthur Walker	#100, 3 3/4"	$900.00
South Bend	#1100B Oreno	$20.00	Arthur Walker	#100 Salmon, 3 3/4"	$1,200.00
South Bend	#1105	$20.00	Wards	#60-6414 Hawthorne, 3 1/4"	$25.00
South Bend	#1110	$20.00	Wards	#61 Auto	$15.00
South Bend	#1115	$20.00	Wards	Precision Auto	$15.00
South Bend	#1120 Orenomatic Auto	$25.00	Weber	#566, Silent Knight	$25.00
South Bend	#1122 Finalist	$25.00	Weber	Kalahatch, 3 3/8"	$30.00
South Bend	#1125 Orenomatic Auto	$20.00	Weber	Trout Reel, 3 1/2"	$15.00
South Bend	#1126 Orenomatic Auto	$20.00	Wells	3" Fly	$100.00
South Bend	#1130D Orenomatic Auto	$25.00	Winchester	#1136 Raised Pillars	$100.00
South Bend	#1140 Orenomatic Auto	$20.00	Winchester	#1135 40-yd.	$120.00
South Bend	#1150 Orenomatic Auto	$20.00	Winchester	#1235 60-yd.	$90.00
South Bend	#1165 Oreno, 3 1/2"	$25.00	Winchester	#1421 80-yd	$50.00
South Bend	#1165 Oreno, Maroon, 3 1/2"	$35.00	Winchester	#1418, Brass	$100.00
South Bend	#1170 St. Joe	$25.00	Yawman & Erbe	Auto (1880 Pat.)	$150.00
South Bend	#1175 Oreno	$20.00	Yawman & Erbe	Auto (1891 Pat.), 3"	$60.00
South Bend	#1180 St. Joe	$20.00	Yawman & Erbe	Auto (1891), 2 1/4"	$60.00
South Bend	#1185	$25.00	J.W. Young	Salmon, Black, 3 1/2"	$90.00
South Bend	#1190	$30.00	J.W. Young	#1505, 3 1/2"	$80.00
South Bend	#1195	$25.00	J.W. Young	#1520, Grey	$50.00
South Bend	(Like Hardy Perfect), 3 5/8"	$70.00	J.W. Young	#1530, 3 1/2"	$100.00
Sport King	#57, 3"	$15.00	J.W. Young	Beaudex Small, 3"	$70.00
Sport King	#64 Auto	$20.00	J.W. Young	Beaudex, Grey, 3 1/2"	$60.00
Sterling		$25.00	J.W. Young	Beaudex, 3 3/4"	$70.00
Tagren	Re-Treev-It	$25.00	J.W. Young	Beaudex, Wireline Guide	$60.00
Terry	1871 Patent, 1 7/8"	$125.00	J.W. Young	Beaudex, 4"	$60.00
Thomas & Thomas	Classic	$230.00	J.W. Young	Condex, 3 1/4"	$55.00
Union Hardware	#7169, 3"	$25.00	J.W. Young	Condex, 3 7/16"	$70.00
Union Hardware	Sunnybrook, Brass	$15.00	J.W. Young	Pridex, 3 1/2"	$60.00
Valentine	89, Disc. Drag	$80.00	J.W. Young	Pridex, 3 3/4"	$60.00
Edward Vom Hofe	#355 Peerless	$2,200.00	J.W. Young	Rapidex, 4"	$125.00
Edward Vom Hofe	#355 Peerless Trout	$2,000.00	J.W. Young	Rapier Graphite, 3 1/4"	$25.00
Edward Vom Hofe	#355 Peerless #3, 2 5/8"	$1,400.00	J.W. Young	Rapier Narrow, 3 3/4"	$25.00
Edward Vom Hofe	#360 Perfection, 2 3/4"	$6,500.00	J.W. Young	Voldex, 3"	$150.00
Edward Vom Hofe	#423, 4"	$1,000.00	J.W. Young & Sons	Ambidex #2	$50.00
Edward Vom Hofe	#423 Salmon	$800.00	J.W. Young & Sons	Beaudex	$75.00
Edward Vom Hofe	#423 (1883) Pat.	$700.00	J.W. Young & Sons	Pridex	$100.00
Edward Vom Hofe	#423 Custom, 3 3/4"	$1,200.00	J.W. Young & Sons	Rapidex	$140.00
Edward Vom Hofe	#504 Tobique	$900.00	J.W. Young & Sons	Seldex	$60.00
Julius Vom Hofe	Raised Pillars	$600.00	Otto Zwarg	#300 Screwhandle, 3 1/2"	$1,200.00
Julius Vom Hofe	Aluminum, 3 3/8"	$500.00	Otto Zwarg	#300 Aluminum Fort, 3 1/2"	$900.00
Julius Vom Hofe	Crown, 3"	$350.00	Otto Zwarg	#300 7 Position Drag, 3 5/8"	$1,000.00
Julius Vom Hofe	Fairy Fly, 2 1/4"	$600.00	Otto Zwarg	#400 Tiny Multiplier	$1,700.00
Von Lengerke & Antoine	Size 3 Fly	$175.00	Otto Zwarg	#400 Multiplier, 3 3/4"	$1,000.00
			Otto Zwarg	#400 Laurentian	$1,500.00
Von Lengerke & Detmold	Hardy Uniqua Style, 2 7/8"	$150.00	Otto Zwarg	#400 Salmon, 3 3/4"	$1,000.00
Walker	#200, Salmon	$1,100.00	Otto Zwarg	Multiplier Salmon, 3 1/2"	$2,000.00

Chapter VII
Reels in Color

New York style ball handle reels – unknown. Values: All are valued in the $500 range.

Top left: Early Von Holfe-type with click and drag button. Value: $400.
Top center: Early New York 1860-1870 with tension button. Value: $300.
Top right: Early convoy type with click button. Value: $500.
Bottom middle: Half handle with tension arm. Value: $300.
Bottom right: Early extra long foot; half handle; tension button. Value: $200.
Bottom left: Early Vom Hofe. Value: $400.
All these reels are mid- to late 1880s, "Origin Unknown."

Vom Hofe reels.
Left: 423 Salmon with detent drag, size 6/0. Value: $900.
Right 423 Salmon, size 4/0. Value: $1,000.

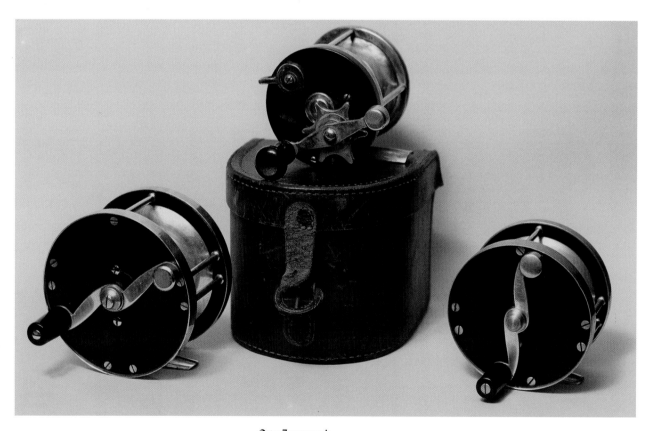

Otto Zwarg reels.
Left: 400 4/0. Value: $1,200.
Center: #1. Value: $1,000.
Right: 400 2/0. Value: $1,500.

Tom Green's cabinet.

Early Leonards.
Left: pat. 1890.
Right: no patent date.
Values: $1,500 each.

Leonard raised pillar with box. Value: $1,200.

Evolution of the New York reels.
Left: Edward Vom Hofe – 1880. Value: $3,500.
Middle: Conroy Makers – half; S-handle, 1865. Value: $5,000.
Right: Julius Vom Hofe – extra long foot; S-handle. Value: $3,500.
These three reels together are valued at over $15,000.00.

Left: Convoy, Bisset Malleson – S-handle. Value: $500.
Center: Thos. J. Conroy Maker – S-handle. Value: $700.
Right: Julius Vom Hofe – Cloverleaf trademark S-handle. Value: $750.
All these reels are circa late 1880s.

Close-up of ratchet mechanism – Julius Vom
Hofe, 1880. Note the fine craftsmanship.

Hardy "Rod in Hand" Perfect – 1898-1902. Value: $1,200.

Hardy fly reels.
Left: Hardy Rod in Hand – white ivory handle; 1898. Value: $1,200.
Middle: Hardy "Uniqua;" size 3 1/2; 1910-1920. Value: $500.
Right: Hardy Perfect; size 3 1/4; 1910-1920. Value: $400.

Left: B.C. Milam #6; half handle. Value: $3,000.
Middle: B.C. Milam #9; Tarpon. Value: $7,500.
Right: B.C. Milam #5. Value: $2,000.

J.L. Sage #3, Frankfort, 1886-1887. Value: $4,000.

Meisselbach bait caster (left) and two views of the famous Tak-a-Part. Values: Baitcaster: $100; Takapart: $150.

Al Foss easy control, possibly by Heddon. Value: $500.

Talbot prem. #1, Nevada. Value: $750.

"Intrinsic" – Wm. Mills & Son. Value: $2,000.

Meek & Milam #0, smallest Meek Milam Kentucky reel ever made. Extremely rare. Value: $10,000.

Yawman & Erbe, first auto fly reel. Value: $150.

Yawman & Erbe – sideview.

A rare A.B. Harthill; Aug. 7, 1866. Value: $1,200.

Vom Hofe "Perfection" size #1, rare size; 1883. Value: $2,500.

Early Edw. Vom Hofe; click & drag button. Value: $1,200.

The very rare Holzman with wraparound perforation
half sleeve. Valued at $5,000.00. 1902 ex-small.

Meek & Milam #0 compared to a Meek & Milam #9 Tarpon.
Values: Milam #0: $5,000-$10,000; Milam #9: $5,000.

Meek & Milam #0 and Meek & Milam #1 with three numbered screws.
Values: left: over $5,000, very rare; right: $2,500. The lure is not for sale.

Pflueger Supreme 1st model. Value: $750.

Pflueger Supreme 1st model showing level wind mechanism.

Benjamin Wisner reels, very rare.
Both narrow and wide spool
models are valued at $5,000.

Benjamin Wisner reels from the side, note the intricate machine work.

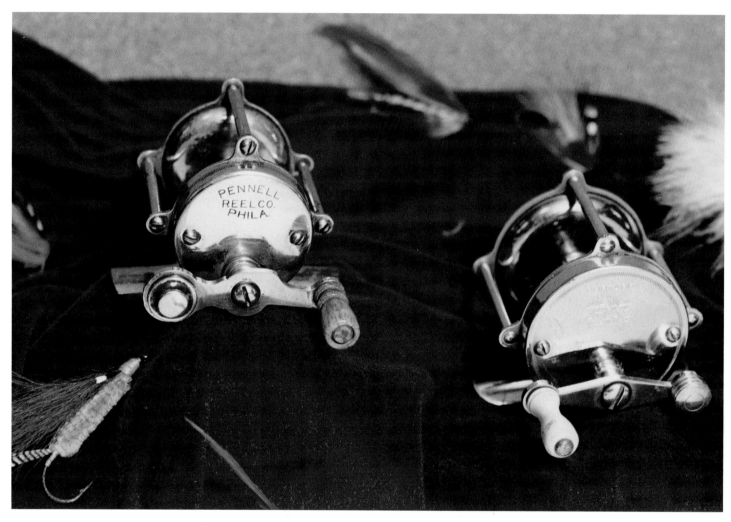

Two cheap raised pillar punched metal reels of the early twentieth century.
Left: Pennell. Value: $50.
Right: Atlas Portage. Value: $50.

Low priced reels of the mid-twentieth century.
Left. Zebro Streamlite. Value: $75.
Right: Horrocks-Ibbotson Commodore. Value: $30.

A trio of fly reels.
Left: The RE-TREEVE-IT by Pachner & Koller, Inc. A fly reel that allowed
retrieval by finger pressure on the lever. Value: $30.
Middle: Meek #56 by Horton. Value: $100.
Right: Pflueger Medalist. Value: $50.

Automatic fly reels.
Left: Pflueger Superex; 1907 patent. Value: $40.
Middle: Shakespeare #1837. Value: $40.
Right: Perrine Auto No. 80 by Alladin Labs, Minneapolis. Value: $20.

Finnor – Wedding Cake; #1, #3. Values: left: $1,000; right: $1,000.

Hardy Fortuna, 7". Value: $1,500.

Left: Pflueger Medalist; Pflueger early Progress trout reel, popular in the 1920s. Values: left: $120; right: $75.

Left: Pflueger Medalist, large size. Value: $140.
Right: Meisselbach punched fly reel, pat. Feb. 32, 1986. Value: $50.

Shakespeare "Beetzel." Value: $450.

Shakespeare Sportcast direct drive. Value: $30.

Left: Shakespeare "Marhoff" model GE. Value: $50.
Right: Shakespeare No. 1924 direct drive. Value: $50.

Left: Pflueger Skilcast No. 1953. Value: $40.
Right: Pflueger Summit No. 1993 L. Value: $40.

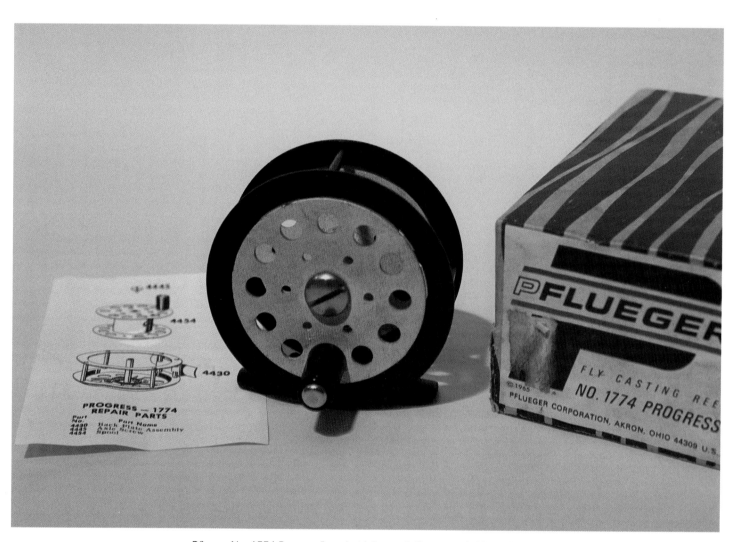

Pflueger No. 1774 Progress fly reel with box and all paperwork. Value: $25.

Appendix I
Care and Maintenance of Collectible Reels

Maintaining old collectible reels is no different than servicing modern reel tackle. We do have the added advantage of highly penetrating oil mediums and miracle greases to make maintenance both easier and more efficient.

In this section I will touch upon some valid and sound procedures that should assist the reader in the care and maintenance of rare reels, as well as reels of all types.

Lubricants: There are a myriad of oils and grease types for all applications. The following are my select choices, the ones I rely on exclusively.

Machine oils: These go back to the earlier days and are still worthy contenders. Sewing machine oil is a prime example: a good, strong, highly efficient lubricant.

Atlas Motor Bearing Lube™: Unless you are a fellow model railroader, this medium will be totally foreign to you. It is made for the delicate gearing in H.O. locomotives, but I find it an excellent, slightly viscous lubricant ideal for old (and new) reel gearing mechanisms.

Atlas Gear Lubricant™: The #190 is the "reel" choice here, great for gears. It is a more viscous type that is applied with a small brush or toothpick. As it is not as penetrating as the aforementioned, it is recommended that excess lube is wiped off. If you can see globs of lube around the gears, you have applied too much.

La Belle #107™: This is a highly efficient and versatile lubricating oil of medium oil viscosity recommended for fishing reels. It is non-drying, non-sludging, and non-staining, coupled with a low evaporation weight.

La Belle #108™: This is another multi-purpose oil, but of a thinner consistency than #107. Formulated for timing mechanisms, miniature motors, and precision instrument gearing, it is a select lubricant for the finer mechanisms of precision reels.

Appendix II
Major Reel Tackle Manufacturers

Abercrombie & Fitch
New York, New York

Franklin Alger
Grand Rapids, Michigan

American Rod & Gun
Stamford, Connecticut

Fred Arbogast Co. Inc.
Akron, Ohio.

Barr-Royer
Waterloo, Iowa

Bristol Rods (Horton Mfg.)
Bristol, Connecticut

Bronson Reel Co.
Bronson, Michigan

Chicago Tackle Co.
Chicago, Illinois

Harry Comstock
Fulton, New York

Ans. B. Decker
Lake Hopatcong, New Jersey

George Gayle & Sons
Frankfort, Kentucky

Gladding Corp. (South Bend)
Syracuse, New York

Helin Tackle Co.
Troy, Michigan

Horrocks-Ibbotson Co.
Utica, New York

Hiram L. Leonard
Bangor, Maine

E.C. Meacham Arms Co.
St. Louis, Missouri

Abbey & Imbrie
New York, New York

Alliance Mfg. Co.
Alliance, Ohio

Anglers Supply Co.
Utica, New York

Associated Specialties
Chicago, Illinois

Thomas H. Bate & Co.
New York, New York

Broadcaster Lures
Youngstown, Ohio

Julio Buel
Whitehall, New York

Thomas H. Chubb
Post Mills, Vermont

Thomas J. Conroy
New York, New York

H & D Folsom Arms Co.
New York, New York

General Merchandise Co.
Milwaukee, Wisconsin

James Heddon & Sons
Dowagiac, Michigan

Hibbard, Spencer, Bartlett
Chicago, Illinois

Horton Mfg. Co.
Bristol, Connecticut

Martin Automatic Fishing Reel Co.
Mohawk, New York

B.F. Meek & Sons, Inc.
Louisville, Kentucky

A.F. Meisselbach & Brothers
Newark, New Jersey

H. H. Michaelson
Brooklyn, New York

William Mills & Son
Central Valley, New York

Robert Ogilvy Co.
New York, New York

W.E. Oster Mfg.
Chicago, Illinois

F.A. Pardee & Co.
Kent, Ohio

Pflueger Sporting Goods
Columbia, South Carolina

Rawlings Sporting Goods Co.
St. Louis, Missouri

Shakespeare Co.
Columbia, South Carolina

Stockford Reel Co.
Chicago, Illinois

Fred E. Thomas
Bangor, Maine

Edward Vom Hofe & Co.
New York, New York

Von Lengerke & Detmold
New York, New York

Wilkinson Co.
Chicago, Illinois

Winchester Arms Co.
New Haven, Connecticut

Yawman & Erbe
Rochester, New York

Mermade Bait Co.
Platteville, Wisconsin

B.C. Milam
Frankfort, Kentucky

New York Sporting Goods Co.
New York, New York

Orvis Co.
Manchester, Vermont

Outing Mfg. Co.
Elkhart, Indiana

Paw Paw Bait Co.
Paw Paw, Michigan

Phillips Fly & Tackle Co.
Alexandria, Pennsylvania

Rider Casting Reel Co.
Ft. Wayne, Indiana

Shapleigh Hardware Co.
St. Louis, Missouri

Talbot Reel & Mfg. Co.
Kansas City, Missouri

Trenton Fishing Tackle
Covington, Kentucky

Von Lengerke & Antoine
Chicago, Illinois

Weber Tackle Co.
Stevens Point, Wisconsin

Thomas E. Wilson & Co.
New York City, Chicago, San Francisco

Wright & McGill
Denver, Colorado

Reel Values

The key to the value of the reel is:

A: Its rarity.
B: Its cosmetic condition.
C: Its flawless operation.

The National Fishing Lure Collectors Association has tried to clarify quality by means of a grading which, at best, can be hit and miss according to individual judgments. Value guides must take into account current trends, reel item availability, current selling prices, comparable sale prices in antique tackle shops, tackle shows, tackle auctions, and collector/dealer lists. Antique shops may intermittently feature tackle, but their prices tend to be on the high side.

Reel Condition

The condition of the reel is the main key to its value as a collectible piece. First and foremost, it should be comprised of all its original parts. This includes the screws and pins that hold the reel together. Replacement parts, though not affecting the function, devalue a reel. If, perchance, you may come upon defunct reels or optional parts that match the original issue and the replacement is not detectable, the reel can retain its value.

The reel must function well mechanically; the spool must turn easily, the gears engage readily, and drag and click mechanisms sound. Sometimes a basic cleaning and lubrication with one or all of the lubricants mentioned in this appendix will bring a reel back to almost new condition. Avoid reels with a damaged gear train, bent pillars and dented frames.

Great attention is paid to the cosmetic appearance of a reel by collectors and buyers. Beware of reels, brass or nickel, that are highly shined. This means that the reel was highly cleaned or polished with an abrasive metal cleaner, which can wear down the surface. Polishing may remove the original patina of the reel, which, in turn, will diminish its value. Finishes should be left untouched to preserve their value. Oil, refined oil, is the only element that should be introduced into the reel. Worn surfaces garnish a proportionate reduction in overall value.

Rusting and pitting can prevail on very old reels, especially if used in or around salt water. If this has occurred, **never** scrape or wire-brush it off. A mild rust remover or inhibitor may lessen the problem and inhibit recurrence; however, it will never completely resolve the ravaged situation. Simple dirt or grease are never major problems; either can be easily removed with a good cleansing with mild oil soap or automotive liquid wax and grease remover.

The Reel Grading System

Mint: Never used and hardly handled. Value escalates if original box and paperwork in mint condition are available.

Excellent: Sometimes phrased "Near Mint" by collectors, denotes a reel that shows minimal cosmetic or mildly discernable flaws. It must exhibit infrequent use and be mechanically functional.

Very Good: Exhibiting average use and wear, some cosmetic aging, minor flaws (scratches, etc.), and no operational defects.

Good: Still fully functional, good appearance, minor rust and pitting, some gear wear, and worn surface plating.

Fair: In this category there are some extremes in judgment. Escapes the good character with more than minor cosmetic appeal; maybe some structural shortcomings.

Poor: Poor reels are best reserved for the spare parts category and are demeaned by their bad or ravaged appearance, broken and missing parts, and ill- or non-functioning mechanical parts. Poor has only nostalgic value.

Major Collectible Reel Values
$500 and Upwards

Manufacturer	Name: Model #	Values	Manufacturer	Name: Model #	Values
Abbey & Imbrie	#2 JVH	$595.00	Hardy	St. George Jr. 2-9/16" Fly	$700.00
Abel	Bluewater, size 5	$1,000.00	Hardy	Davy reel, brass	$2,500.00
Abu	Ambassador #5000	$600.00	Hardy	Zane Grey 6"	$3,000.00
API	Anti Reverse Reel-3-3/4"	$525.00	Haywood	1-5/8" brass clamp	$500.00
T.H. Bate & Co.	1-7/8" Ball handle	$5,350.00	C.R. Klein	Aluminum	$950.00
Thomas Bate	Brass model	$1,450.00	Kosmic	#821	$650.00
Benjamin	Thumezy	$500.00	Kovalovsky	Zane Grey	$6,000.00
Billinghurst	Birdcage, 1859	$12,000.00	Kovalovsky	Blue Water	$550.00
Billinghurst	3-1/2" 1859	$1,600.00	Kovalovsky	Searlin	$500.00
Billinghurst	Brass Birdcage	$1,540.00	Kovalovsky	#1250	$1,500.00
Billinghurst	Fly, 1859	$795.00	Kovalovsky	#51	$1,025.00
Bluegrass Reel Works	#3	$850.00	Kovalovsky	#91	$1,175.00
Bluegrass Reel Works	#3 jewel handle	$595.00	Kentucky Bluegrass	#3	$600.00
Bogdan	Baby, wide spool	$1,900.00	Kentucky Bluegrass	#4 extra rare	$675.00
Bogdan	3-1/4" Fly	$1,100.00	Leonard	Light Salmon	$575.00
Bogdan	Salmon Multiplyer	$1,600.00	Leonard-Mills	Midge 2-3/8"	$1,200.00
Bogdan	Baby Trout Reel		Hil. Leonard	2-3/8" bronze	$2,500.00
	Silver 2-1/4" x 1/8"	$1,550.00	Hil. Leonard	2-3/8"	$2,500.00
Bradford & Anthony	Brass 1860	$1,050.00	Hil. Leonard	2-5/8"	$850.00
Bradford & Anthony	1860 2/0	$800.00	Hil. Leonard	191813	$1,600.00
Boston Bradford	2", 1850	$900.00	Hil. Leonard	Bi-metal	$1,395.00
Carlton Mfg. Co.	Bait Caster	$650.00	Hil. Leonard	Trout Click Reel	$1,650.00
Carpenter & Casey	#1 N, 2-5/8"	$550.00	Master Kaster	#2	$725.00
Chubbs	Black Bass Reel	$4,750.00	Master Kaster	#3	$725.00
Clerk & Co.	#5 Fly	$600.00	Medley's	#3 20th Cent.	$3,000.00
C.M. Clinton	Side Mount Fly	$4,300.00	Meek & Milam	#1	$3,200.00
A. Coates	multiplyer	$600.00	Meek & Milam	#2 1860	$1,800.00
J.A. Coxe	14/0	$1,250.00	Meek & Milam	#2 1855	$1,600.00
J.A. Coxe	9/0	$650.00	Meek & Milam	#2 ball handle	$1,045.00
J.A. Coxe	Big Game	$600.00	Meek & Milam	#2 bass 1870	$1,200.00
J.A. Coxe	Zane Grey	$1,300.00	Meek & Milam	#2 bone handle	$1,100.00
J. Deally	#10	$3,700.00	Meek & Milam	#2 brass, half-handle	$1,400.00
J. Deally	#2	$2,300.00	Meek & Milam	#3 1870	$1,000.00
J. Dreiser	4-1/4"	$900.00	Meek & Milam	#3-1/2 handle	$1,050.00
John Emery	4-3/8" Fly	$1,500.00	Meek & Milam	#4 numbered screws	$1,200.00
John Emery	3-7/8" Fly	$1,700.00	B.F. Meek	#2 brass	$3,000.00
Fin-Nor	#2	$1,150.00	B.F. Meek	#3 Tournament	$1,000.00
Fin-Nor	Wedding Cake 3" Fly	$1,150.00	B.F. Meek & Sons	#2 Tournament	$600.00
Fin-Nor	Garwood	$1,150.00	B.F. Meek & Sons	#3 Free-spool	$660.00
Flint Reel Co.	The Michigan	$8,500.00	B.F. Meek & Sons	#44	$3,900.00
Follet	Fly	$1,400.00	B.F. Meek & Sons	#5 Bluegrass	$750.00
Follet	Bird Cage Fly	$725.00	B.F. Meek & Sons	#7	$2,550.00
Follet	side mount 3-5/8" Trout	$500.00	B.F. Meek & Sons	#8	$2,600.00
Alonso Fowler	GEM	$4,000.00	B.F. Meek & Sons	Club Special	$2,250.00
G.W. Gayle & Son	2-1/4" Trout	$8,500.00	J.F. and B.F. Meek	Unnumbered early	$7,750.00
G.W. Gayle & Son	#3 Frankfort, KY	$1,200.00	Milam	#1	$2,500.00
G.W. Gayle & Son	Tarpon, handmade	$3,500.00	B.C. Milam	#2	$1,000.00
Ted Godfrey	Restigonche Salmon	$550.00	B.C. Milam	#2 pendulum handle	$1,110.00
Hardy	Birmingham Plate 2-1/2" Fly	$1,000.00	B.C. Milam	#2 Frankfort	$1,200.00
Hardy	Bougle 1920 3" Fly	$1,650.00	B.C. Milam	#3 Frankfort	$1,200.00
Hardy	Bougle Fly 3-1/4"	$1,750.00	B.C. Milam	#3 1880	$1,200.00
Hardy	Cascabedia Fly 2"	$3,600.00	B.C. Milam	limited horseshoe Ed.	$900.00
Hardy	Cascapedia 7-7 position drag	$5,900.00	B.C. Milam	1/2 handle, buffalo knob	$2,500.00
Hardy	Cascapedia 3-5/8" Fly	$3,900.00	Wm. Mills & Son	#2 pearl knob	$1,200.00
Hardy	Hercules	$600.00	Wm. Mills & Son	Leonard Fairy Trout	$1,100.00
Hardy	Hercules, bronze	$1,000.00	Wm. Mills & Son	Leonard Salmon	$550.00
Hardy	Jock Scott	$1,350.00	Wm. Mills & Son	Leonard Mills 3-1/8"	$890.00
Hardy	Perfect-brass faced	$1,200.00	Wm. Mills & Son	4" 1890	$500.00
Hardy	Perfect-wide drum 1905	$750.00	Wm. Mills & Son	Dry Fly	$850.00
Hardy	Perfect-wide drum	$1,400.00	Wm. Mills & Son	Fairy Trout 2"	$1,400.00
Hardy	Perfect-narrow drum 1905-1911	$850.00	Wm. Mills & Son	Intrinsic	$1,200.00
Hardy	Perfect-rare, left handed	$1,100.00	Orris	1874 early model	$620.00
Hardy	St. George 2-9/16" Fly	$575.00	Peerless	#5 Fly	$595.00

Manufacturer	Name: Model #	Values
Peerless	#6 Fly	$595.00
Poss Reels	Heritage Fly	$1,400.00
J.L. Sage	#3	$4,000.00
Seamaster	Dual Mode	$2,400.00
Seamaster	Mark I	$1,500.00
Seamaster	Mark I Baby Doll	$1,750.00
Seamaster	Brass Mark II 4-1/2" Fly	$1,850.00
Seamaster	Mark II black & gold	$1,500.00
Seamaster	Mark IV 4-1/8" Fly	$1,500.00
Seamaster	Mark IV Tarpon	$1,250.00
Seamaster	Salmon (1st model)	$1,850.00
Seamaster	Bone Fish	$1,550.00
Talbot	Tournament	$500.00
Talbot	Tomahawk	$525.00
Talbot Reel & Mfg. Co.	#31	$650.00
Wm. H. Talbot	Eli, Nevada model	$700.00
Wm. H. Talbot	Ben Hur	$5,500.00
Wm. H. Talbot Co.	Niangna model	$400.00
Wm. H. Talbot Co.	#3	$770.00
Edward Vom Hofe	#355 Peerless	$2,200.00
Edward Vom Hofe	#355 Peerless Trout	$2,000.00
Edward Vom Hofe	#355 Peerless #3	$1,400.00
Edward Vom Hofe	#355 Peerless Size 3	$1,250.00
Edward Vom Hofe	#360 Perfection	$6,270.00
Edward Vom Hofe	#423	$1,350.00
Edward Vom Hofe	#423 Special	$950.00
Edward Vom Hofe	#423 Salmon	$2,250.00
Edward Vom Hofe	#423 1902	$1,200.00
Edward Vom Hofe	#423 7 position drag	$700.00
Edward Vom Hofe	#423 name engraved	$695.00
Edward Vom Hofe	#423 Custom	$1,200.00
Edward Vom Hofe	423 Restigouche (1902)	$600.00
Edward Vom Hofe	Restigouche Phlidelphia	$1,195.00
Edward Vom Hofe	#423 Salmon, 7 pos. drag	$1,275.00
Edward Vom Hofe	#429	$525.00
Edward Vom Hofe	#484 Col. Thompson	$1,400.00
Edward Vom Hofe	#491 Universal	$500.00
Edward Vom Hofe	#501	$900.00
Edward Vom Hofe	#504	$2,900.00
Edward Vom Hofe	#504 Superwide	$2,800.00
Edward Vom Hofe	#504 Salmon	$1,050.00
Edward Vom Hofe	#504 wide Salmon	$850.00
Edward Vom Hofe	Salmon Reel	$1,100.00
Edward Vom Hofe	#504 Tobique 1896	$1,165.00
Edward Vom Hofe	#504 Tobique 1902	$2,600.00
Edward Vom Hofe	#504 Tobique multi	$1,250.00
Edward Vom Hofe	#650 Islamorada	$675.00
Edward Vom Hofe	#722 Commander Ross	$1,050.00
Edward Vom Hofe	Peerless Trout Reel	$1,850.00
Edward Vom Hofe	Perfection 1883	$3,200.00
Edward Vom Hofe	#16	$1,200.00
Edward Vom Hofe	#3	$1,450.00
Edward Vom Hofe	#5	$1,050.00
Julius Vom Hofe	Ocean Salmon Reel	$1,300.00
Walker	#200 Salmon	$1,095.00
Walker	TR-1	$1,250.00
Walker	TR-2	$1,000.00
Walker	TR-3	$835.00
Walker	TR-3 Trout	$1,000.00
Walker	#300 Salmon	$975.00
Arthur Walker	3 100	$875.00
Arthur Walker	#100 Salmon	$1,100.00
Otto Zwarg	#300	$1,100.00
Otto Zwarg	#300 3-1/2" X 2	$900.00
Otto Zwarg	#300 7 pos. drag	$950.00
Otto Zwarg	#400 multiplier	$1,750.00
Otto Zwarg	#400 7 pos. drag	$895.00
Otto Zwarg	#400 tiny multiplier	$1,695.00
Otto Zwarg	#Brooklyn	$895.00
Otto Zwarg	#400 Alum. Multiplier	$1,000.00
Otto Zwarg	#400 Larentian	$1,450.00
Otto Zwarg	multiplier Salmon	$1,450.00
Otto Zwarg	Salmon Reel	$1,200.00

Reel Values $100 to $500

Manufacturer	Name: Model #	Values
A & N	Salmon Reel 5"	$110.00
A & N	3" Fly	$175.00
Abbey & Imbrie	GS	$440.00
Abbey & Imbrie	Fly	$100.00
Abbey & Imbrie	Silver King	$200.00
Abel	Fly, adj. Drag	$295.00
Abel	TR-1	$250.00
Abel	TR-2	$335.00
Abel	TR-3	$275.00
Abu	#1750	$120.00
Abu	#1800 Record	$125.00
Abu	#2100 Record	$200.00
Abu	#2100 Record Sport	$450.00
Abu	#2500C Ambassadeur	$150.00
Abu	#4000D	$110.00
Abu	#4000D Ambassadeur	$120.00
Abu	#5000	$125.00
Abu	#5000 DLX Amb.	$350.00
Abu	#5000A Ambassadeur	$135.00
Abu	#5000D Ambassadeur	$110.00
Abu	#5001C Ambassadeur	$100.00
Abu	#5500 Ambassadeur	$140.00
Abu	#5500C	$100.00
Abu	#5600C Ambassadeur	$120.00
Abu	#6000 Ambassadeur	$100.00
Abu	Cardinal 3	$150.00
Abu	Cardinal 33	$150.00
Abu	Cardinal 4	$125.00
Abu	Cardinal 4X	$135.00
Abu	Cardinal 7	$100.00
Abu	Delta 5	$110.00
Abu Record	#1800	$125.00
Abu Record	#6000	$150.00
Alcedo	Mark IV	$100.00
Alcedo	Micron	$100.00
Allcock	Brass Salmon	$135.00
Allcock	#8931 Stanley	$100.00
Allcock	Aerial	$425.00
Allen A.	Spin cast	$220.00
Allison	Salmon	$100.00
AP 1	Spring Creek Ltd.	$400.00
AP 1	Special Ltd. edition	$400.00
AP 1	Spring Creek	$260.00
ATH	F 3	$275.00
ATH	Rio Orbigo	$325.00
Bradford & Anthony	Boston 1860	$450.00
Bradford & Anthony	Salmon Reel	$440.00
Carlton Rochester	MKD Triumph	$175.00
Carpenter & Casey	Trout Reel	$375.00
Carter	Jardine	$210.00
Clerk & Co.	Ball handle 1850	$450.00
Conroy	#1	$200.00
Conroy	#2	$200.00
Conroy	#5	$250.00
J.A. Coxe	#15	$165.00
J.A. Coxe	#25	$135.00
J.A. Coxe	#525	$100.00

Manufacturer	Name: Model #	Values	Manufacturer	Name: Model #	Values
J.A. Coxe	Expert Twenty	$125.00	H.I. Leonard	3-3/8	$195.00
Dingley	Scottie	$350.00	H.I. Leonard	4-1/4" Salmon	$495.00
Dingley	Westly Richards	$195.00	Liberty Bell	#250A	$250.00
Fin-Nor	#1 Trout	$320.00	Liberty Bell	#A	$400.00
Fin-Nor	#2	$275.00	Liberty Bell Reel	C 1900	$300.00
Fin-Nor	#3 Anti Reverse	$295.00	Malloch	various models	$120-270.00
Fin-Nor	#4 Garwood Jr.	$345.00	Meek-Horton	#2	$350.00
Fin-Nor	#4A Tycoon	$325.00	Meek-Horton	#3	$285.00
Fin-Nor	#12 Golden Regal	$195.00	Meek-Horton	#3 Bluegrass	$200.00
Fin-Nor	Model 20 Regal	$220.00	Meek-Horton	#3 model 3 M	$325.00
Fin-Nor	Model 30 Regal	$220.00	Meek-Horton	#3 Freespool	$325.00
Fin-Nor	Model 50 Regal	$245.00	Meek-Horton	#30	$250.00
Four Brothers	Comrade	$145.00	Meek-Horton	#25	$125.00
Four Brothers	Delite (40 yd)	$155.00	Meek-Horton	#33 Simplex	$250.00
Four Brothers	Delite (60 yd)		Meek-Horton	#34 Bluegrass Simplex	$325.00
Four Brothers	Delite (80 yd)	$160.00	Meek	#4 Tournament	$100.00
Frankfort Special	Kn. Style	$325.00	B.F. Meek	#56	$195.00
Hardy	2-1/2" Brim. Trout	$300.00	B.F. Meek	#25 #3 Bluegrass	$245.00
Hardy	Altex	$150.00	B.F. Meek & Sons	#25 (Carter)	$235.00
Hardy	Altex #1 Mark V	$140.00	B.F. Meek & Sons	#25 Bluegrass	$195.00
Hardy	Altex #2 Mark III	$120.00	B.F. Meek & Sons	#3	$350.00
Hardy	Altex #3 Mark V	$150.00	B.F. Meek & Sons	#3 Tournament	$700.00
Hardy	Eureka	$325.00	B.F. Meek & Sons	#33	$275.00
Hardy	Fly weight	$185.00	B.F. Meek & Sons	#33 Bluegrass	$175.00
Hardy	Gem	$180.00	B.F. Meek & Sons	#4 Bluegrass	$350.00
Hardy	Golden Prince	$190.00	Meisselbach	#148	$145.00
Hardy	Husky Salmon	$195.00	Meisselbach	#252 Symblopart	$140.00
Hardy	Longstone	$200.00	Meisselbach	#600 OKEH	$150.00
Hardy	Marquis #10	$110.00	Meisselbach	#780 Tripart	$150.00
Hardy	Marquis #5	$120.00	Mepps	Super Meca	$100.00
Hardy	Perfect series	$120-350.00	Wm. Mills & Co.	G.S. Multiplier	$355.00
Haskell	2-3/4" Fly	$475.00	Wm. Mills & Co.	Salmon	$150.00
Haskell	3-3/8" Fly	$425.00	Mitchell	Big Game	$190.00
Heddon	#125 Imperial	$195.00	Mitchell	#301 D L	$300.00
Heddon	#3-15	$225.00	Montaque	Fly	$165.00
Heddon	#3-25	$300.00	Montaque	#12 Imperial	$125.00
Heddon	#3-35	$300.00	Montaque	#9 Imperial	$100.00
Heddon	#3-45 (Carter)	$250.00	Ocean City	#300	$115.00
Heddon	#30 Sea & Lake	$125.00	Ocean City	#609	$150.00
Heddon	#30 Winona	$100.00	Ocean City	#609 Long Key	$175.00
Heddon	#3015	$175.00	Ocean City	Balboa	$230.00
Heddon	#45	$350.00	Ocean City	Long Key	$130.00
Heddon	#P41 L	$135.00	Ocean City	Orlando	$190.00
Heddon	Great Lakes	$200.00	Ocean City	Takapart	$125.00
Heddon & Sons	#3-15	$200.00	Orvis	#100A	$125.00
Heddon & Sons	#3-35	$225.00	Orvis	#175	$120.00
Heddon & Sons	#45	$450.00	Orvis	#200	$115.00
Hendryx	Alum. Fly	$120.00	Orvis	1874 Model	$325.00
Holiday	#30	$100.00	Orvis	Batten Kill Mark V	$110.00
Holiday	#40	$100.00	Orvis	CFO 123	$120.00
Horrocks-Ibbotson	#1	$250.00	Orvis	CFO II Barstock	$135.00
Horton	#3 Bluegrass	$250.00	Orvis	CFO IV	$125.00
Horton	#3 KY Bluegrass	$195.00	Orvis	Commemorative 1874	$375.00
Horton	#33 KY Bluegrass	$110.00	Orvis	DXR	$220.00
Horton	#33 Bluegrass Simplex	$175.00	Orvis	Presentation EXR II	$220.00
Horton	#34 Bluegrass	$450.00	Orvis	Presentation EXR III	$125.00
Horton	#4 KY Bluegrass	$495.00	Orvis	Presentation EXR IV	$165.00
Horton-Meek	#2	$360.00	Orvis	Presentation EXR V	$140.00
Horton-Meek	#25 Bluegrass Simplex	$300.00	Penn	#115 Senator	$100.00
Horton-Meek	#3	$325.00	Penn	#2 Int'l.	$115.00
Horton-Meek	#30	$300.00	Penn	#259 M	$200.00
Horton-Meek	#4	$350.00	Penn	#25 M	$100.00
Horton-Meek	#54	$135.00	Penn	#26 M	$100.00
Horton-Meek	#55	$100.00	Penn	#349 HC	$125.00
Horton-Meek	#56	$115.00	Penn	#M 20 Int'l.	$275.00
Hunter	Kentucky Style	$375.00	Penn	Senator	$275.00
Iver-Johnson	Hardy Uniqua	$125.00	Penn	Senator (Red)	$165.00
Iver-Johnson	Hardy Perfect	$160.00	Perez	#1	$275.00

Manufacturer	Name: Model #	Values	Manufacturer	Name: Model #	Values
Perez	#1 MKD	$165.00	Terry	1871 Pat.	$125.00
Perez	#1 Surf	$100.00	The Kosmic Reel		$325.00
Perez	#50	$320.00	Triumph	1910 Par.	$175.00
Perez	Wondereel	$235.00	Trowbridge	all brass Fly	$125.00
Pflueger	#1134 Golden West		Vom Hofe	#491	$145.00
Pflueger	#Templar	$125.00	Vom Hofe	Salmon, 1902	$350.00
Pflueger	#1433 J	$195.00	Vom Hofe	#1 Universal	$500.00
Pflueger	#1492 Medalist	$120.00	Vom Hofe	#295	$350.00
Pflueger	#1494 Medalist	$195.00	Edw. Vom Hofe	#333 Tarpon	$400.00
Pflueger	#1496 Medalist	$140.00	Edw. Vom Hofe	#521	$200.00
Pflueger	#1592 Medalist	$175.00	Edw. Vom Hofe	#548	$360.00
Pflueger	#182 X Worth	$154.00	Edw. Vom Hofe	#550	$295.00
Pflueger	#1907 Ohio	$150.00	Edw. Vom Hofe	#560 Beach Haven	$470.00
Pflueger	#2479 Autopia	$125.00	Edw. Vom Hofe	#621 1902 Pat.	$350.00
Pflueger	#264 Hawkeye	$210.00	Edw. Vom Hofe	#621 Universal	$340.00
Pflueger	#578 Supreme	$175.00	Julius Vom Hofe	#2	$225.00
Pflueger	Adams	$275.00	Julius Vom Hofe	#2 Multiplier	$110.00
Pflueger	Advance	$100.00	Julius Vom Hofe	#2 Trout	$200.00
Pflueger	Akron, tin case	$375.00	Julius Vom Hofe	#3	$325.00
Pflueger	Atlapac	$300.00	Julius Vom Hofe	#3 Silver King	$180.00
Pflueger	Buckeye	$150.00	Julius Vom Hofe	#3-1/2"	$200.00
Pflueger	Redifor	$130.00	Julius Vom Hofe	#396 1882 Pat.	$110.00
Wm. Read & Sons	Trout	$195.00	Julius Vom Hofe	#4 1885 Pat.	$165.00
Redifor	Beetzel	$350.00	Julius Vom Hofe	#4 quadruple 1889 Pat.	$100.00
Redifor-Beelzel	1906 & 1911 pat.	$400.00	Julius Vom Hofe	#4 baitcaster	$120.00
Carlton Rochester	M K D Triumph	$175.00	Julius Vom Hofe	B. Ocean	$300.00
Scientific Angler	II model	$185.00	Julius Vom Hofe	H-1 #1	$250.00
Scientific Angler	SYS 11	$145.00	Julius Vom Hofe	Midge Reel	$225.00
Scientific Angler	SYS 5	$140.00	Julius Vom Hofe	Pre B-Ocean	$385.00
Scientific Angler	SYS 8	$195.00	Julius Vom Hofe	President 1892 Pat.	$250.00
Scientific Angler	SYS 4	$105.00	Julius Vom Hofe	Size 3"	$225.00
Scientific Angler	SYS 6	$120.00	Julius Vom Hofe	Size 3-1/2"	$160.00
Scientific Angler	SYS II	$135.00	Von Lengert & Detmold	Hardy Uniqua	$135.00
Shakespeare	#1740	$115.00			
Shakespeare	#1740 Tournament	$110.00	Von Lengert & Detmold	3-1/2"	$135.00
Shakespeare	#1743 Tournament	$210.00			
Shakespeare	#1756 Surf Tournament	$250.00	Wells	3" Fly	$100.00
Shakespeare	#1900 Steelhead	$100.00	Wilkie	1895 Pat.	$350.00
Shakespeare	#2210 II Cutaway	$150.00	Winchester	#1135	$110.00
Shakespeare	#24043 Tournament	$140.00	Winchester	#1336	$120.00
Shakespeare	Beetzel 1918	$225.00	Winchester	#2242	$110.00
Shakespeare	Miller Autocrat	$375.00	Winchester	#2342 Crusader	$125.00
Shakespeare	model B 1910	$250.00	Winchester	#2626	$130.00
Shakespeare	Professional #2	$125.00	Winchester	#2730	$120.00
Shakespeare	Professional 1910	$120.00	Winchester	#2744	$110.00
Shakespeare	L.W. Reel #3	$195.00	Winchester	#4240 Takapart	$125.00
Shakespeare	#2 Service	$100.00	Winchester	#4250 Takapart	$125.00
Wm. Shakespeare, Jr.	Crescent	$125.00	Winchester	#4290	$100.00
Wm. Shakespeare, Jr.	Std. Professional	$120.00	Winchester	#4350	$135.00
Wm. Shakespeare, Jr.	Vom Hofe pat. 1910	$250.00	Winchester	#4350 Takapart	$150.00
A.B. Shipley & Sons	#4	$420.00	Winchester	#4356 1920 Pat.	$145.00
M.A. Shipley	Brass	$180.00	Winchester	Freedex	$135.00
South Bend	1390-A	$120.00	J.W. Young	Freedex	$135.00
South Bend	#850 Perfectoreno	$115.00	J.W. Young	Landex	$130.00
South Bend	#1131	$145.00	J.W. Young	Rapidex	$125.00
Stadler Merit	bait-spin reel	$195.00	J.W. Young	Valdex	$140.00
Stockford Reel Co.	Chicago 1910 (scarce)	$375.00	J.W. Young & Sons	Rapidex, Eng.	$130.00
Talbot	#33	$390.00	Zebco	Cardinal 3	$130.00
Talbot	Comet	$400.00	Zebco	Cardinal 4	$125.00
Talbot	Meteor	$300.00	Otto Zwarg	#1600	$269.00
Talbot	Star	$300.00	Otto Zwarg	2/0 Trolling Reel	$360.00
			Otto Zwarg	3/0 Trolling Reel	$330.00